ABHISHEK BACHCHAN

Style & Substance

ABHISHEK BACHCHAN

Style & Substance

PRADEEP CHANDRA

NIYOGI
BOOKS

Published by
NIYOGI BOOKS
D-78, Okhla Industrial Area, Phase-I
New Delhi-110 020, India
Tel: 91-11-26816301, 49327000
Fax: 91-11-26810483, 26813830
Email: niyogibooks@gmail.com
Website: www.niyogibooksindia.com

Editorial and Design: Write Media
ISBN: 978-93-85285-29-5
Year of Publication: 2016

Printed at: Niyogi Offset Pvt. Ltd., New Delhi, India

Dedicated to

Dr Ram Jawhrani

Chairman

Sahyog Foundation

Global Sindhi Council

ALL STARS

Contents

An Ember from the Same Fire

FOREWORD | Malavika Sangghvi

Universally regarded as the most approachable and friendly Bachchan, Abhishek is an example of someone whose singular approach to his life and career has been validated after many years of uncertainty.

Consider the circumstance of his debut: the son of the film industry's biggest star, the inheritor of remarkable acting talent from both his illustrious parents, Jaya and Amitabh Bachchan, a boy who had grown up on the sets watching his famous father, was launched not in a home production, as is the norm in the industry for star sons, but in an outside production and that, too, not one of the big established production studios.

The vehicle that was to launch Abhishek's career was *Refugee*, produced and directed by JP Dutta, best known for patriotic films with war themes. That Dutta's previous film, *Border*, had been a box office hit that was appreciated by the critics as well must have encouraged Abhishek. Yet there was no question that, not only was he choosing to go out on a limb by not debuting in a film produced by his family, he had also chosen one that bucked conventional wisdom. Tradition had it that stars—especially star sons—debuted in love stories predicated on the plot of boy meets girl, boy loses girl and so on. Rishi Kapoor, son of Raj Kapoor, had done that with *Bobby*; Rajendra Kumar's son, Kumar Gaurav, had followed the same path in *Love Story*. Then why on earth was Abhishek, blessed with good looks and a winning personality, who was the apple of his parents' eye, and someone educated in the finest educational institutions across the world, opting for such a risky start to his career?

The answer to that was one word—timing.

Four years before he chose to make his debut with *Refugee*, Abhishek's father had launched his entertainment conglomerate ABCL, the industry's first corporate entity, with mega ambitions to produce and distribute movies, television software, manage events and undertake a host of other activities. But, for one reason or the other, it had come to naught; with films flopping, legal battles mounting, by 1999, ABCL was declared a failed company with the courts even restraining the Bachchans from selling their home, Prateeksha, until their monies were recovered by creditors!

Seen in this light, Abhishek's choice to make his film debut in an outside production, with none of his parent's legendary clout behind him, becomes understandable. He had little choice. His family was facing one of its darkest periods and, at 24, unlike most star sons, Abhishek had to face harsh reality. There was no one in his family in a position to attend to his career at that moment, given that they were in fire-fighting mode themselves. Another man might have balked or turned bitter, but not Abhishek. Displaying the courage that his celebrated father is famous for, he seized the moment, threw caution to the wind and bit the bullet.

I recall going to interview him at Prateeksha, shortly after the release of his first film, for a cover story for *The Times of India*'s Sunday supplement, which at that time I was editing. *Refugee* had not been a box office success, but Abhishek's performance, as the brooding and intense refugee, had been well received and it had won him the industry's Holy Grail: a Filmfare nomination for Best Male Debut. Unconventional and different he may have been, but that he could act and command the attention of the audience had been established.

But, yoked to his surname, that would not be enough. The industry wanted more. Much more. They were looking for the next superstar. It was not enough that the young man had his acting chops: Could he dance? Fight? Ride bareback on horses? Enter the villain's den jump-kick 20 heavies, rescue his blind mother, deliver a patriotic speech, sing a song to the heroine and come out on the other side with a wink and a flop of his hair?

It appeared that Abhishek might have trod too close to the road less taken. His choice of post-debut films was enigmatic, risky and we were concerned. I recall gently trying to convey to Abhishek that perhaps he might want to tread the beaten path. Buy into norm. Walk the party line. It was, after all, an era when his contemporaries were flaunting their hairless torsos and pelvic thrusts, their biceps and newfound swag, and here was Junior B, resolutely unaffected by it all. He did not gym, he was not known for his sartorial flair and he gave little care to his appearance or his image. (He'd appeared for the interview and the photo shoot, for instance, just as he'd been at home, stubble on his chin, barely combed hair, casual.) Didn't he feel the need to shape up, employ hair gel, get a fancy cut, hit the gym, hire a stylist and so on, we asked.

I remember even then, such was Abhishek's confidence and conviction, that I saw an ember smoulder in his eyes. 'Malavika Aunty,' he said, politely but firmly, 'I am an actor, not a bodybuilder. I am here to act, not be known for my looks or my hairstyle or my body. What does that have to do with acting? And where else in the world are actors expected to be like that?' he added, suddenly animated. Once more, Abhishek had displayed his quiet determination and confidence in himself, regardless of convention or norm. Out of respect for his steely determination, we had carried his picture, as he was, ordinary shirt, no styling, hardly any backdrop, the way he had wanted. And, unsurprisingly, we titled the story, 'An ember from the same fire'.

It would have been fitting, of course, if such determination and conviction had been rewarded and Abhishek's iconoclastic belief in himself and the films he wanted to make had been rewarded soon. But that was not to be. In the meantime, his father's fortunes picked up stratospherically. The senior Bachchan had not only starred in Yash Chopra's blockbuster *Mohabbatein*, but he had also made his enormously successful small screen debut with 'Kaun Banega Crorepati', a series that turned his fortunes around dramatically. In contrast, Abhishek's career appeared to be floundering with a tranche of post-debut misguidedly chosen turkeys.

It wasn't until 2004, when he turned in one of his best performances in Mani Ratnam's *Yuva* in which his role as the impassioned and intemperate Lallan in an ensemble cast including Ajay Devgn and Vivek Oberoi won him many accolades. It was also to be the year that saw him embark on an enterprise that worked like the ideal vehicle for his triumphant ride into the box office stakes with the Yash Raj Films' money-spinning *Dhoom* capers—a happy little asset for the Abhishek fortunes. It was around this time that Abhishek stepped out from under the looming banyan tree that he'd been born under and came into his own.

From 2004 there was no looking back for Abhishek. Not only had he survived with sheer grit and remarkable sanguinity one of the bleakest post-debut phases of any actor's life, he had also survived an unfortunate and very public break-up with a leading actress, not allowing it to dampen his enthusiasm or his naturally sunny disposition. And, more important, he was popular among his colleagues and co-stars and loved by all. The fact that he delivered the year's biggest hit, *Bunty Aur Babli*, an edgy (by the standards of those

Amitabh and Abhishek share a special bond.

days) happy little tale of a modern day B-town Bonny and Clyde, the following year clearly established that Abhishek Bachchan was what was referred to as a '*lambi* race *ka ghoda*' [in for the long run]. His marriage to Aishwarya Rai, the industry's darling and considered one of the world's most beautiful women, added the extra sheen on an already gilded image. His father was now back to being the emperor of the industry, the family was one of the most respected in the country, its financial situation had taken a dramatic turn for the better and, all in all, things were moving at a happy trot.

It's been 10 years since *Bunty Aur Babli* and these years have seen Abhishek act in over 30 films. There have been those such as *Umrao Jaan* and *Sarkar* in which his performances have been truly exceptional, achieving pitch perfection in a way that comes close to those of the likes of Dilip Kumar and his own father. His nuanced, textured portrayal of an industrialist in *Guru*, loosely based on Dhirubhai Ambani, displayed what a fine, sensitive and understated actor he could be, getting under the skin of the character while playing a much older man. And in films such as *Dostana* and *Bluffmaster* he has demonstrated a splendid comic timing. Farah Khan, the director of one of his career's biggest hits, *Happy New Year*, believes that he has one of the best talents for comedy in the industry today. 'There is no one who can match his timing and his ability to make even the most inane scene hilarious, if required,' she observes, going on to add, 'Besides, he's one of the most lovable, madcap and affectionate actors in the business today.'

The sentiment is shared by most who have worked with Abhishek; in fact, a brief perusal of his filmography reveals that he is perhaps one of the most 'repeated' actors of his generation. Remarkably, he has done five films with Ram Gopal Varma, four with Apoorva Lakhia, four with Rohan Sippy, three with Mani Ratnam as also with Shaad Ali, JP Dutta, Goldie Behl, Yash Raj Films and Dharma. If repetition is the benchmark of popularity, then Abhishek is the gold star. Ask anyone what he is like to work with and unanimously there is a smile. 'He's a riot,' is what they say. But it is not only in his career that Abhishek has made huge strides. His personal life displays his maturity and sanguinity. No scandals, no tantrums on sets, no drunken binges or intemperate remarks and yet he is no pushover or saint. Abhishek has carved his own path in filmdom today. His image is of a high-spirited, zany, full of mischief and droll humour, loving, responsible actor, husband, father and son. And, as the cherry on the cake, he has expanded his scope to other fields, becoming a brand ambassador, a spokesperson for good causes and now a budding sports entrepreneur with his kabbadi league.

I recall one evening spent at Prateeksha with him, his parents and sister Shweta, which most epitomises Abhishek's personality for me. There was good wine, the mood was mellow and over gentle conversation we assembled at the dining table. Abhishek must have been in his late teens then. He was narrating an incident that had occurred recently on an international flight when the siblings were flying back from school. In the seat next to theirs had been a Caucasian giant, who, when the fasten seatbelt signs had been switched off, had stretched his arms expansively, loosened his collar and placed his heavy boot-enclosed feet on the seat ahead of him, which had collapsed under the weight. Unfortunately and unknown to him, the seat was occupied by a vertically challenged, tiny individual.

Abhishek narrated all this in vivid detail, conjuring up the scene and conveying its essential humour. 'The man in front just went "eee",' he said, making a face. And, for some reason, the face and the sound made us all giggle a lot. Chuffed by the laughter, Abhishek began to narrate other such stories and the gathering, more accustomed to discussions with gravitas, instantly loosened up and began to see the funnier side of things. I recall glancing at Amitabh that evening, as his young son became the centre of attention. I saw a look of such bursting paternal pride that it has stayed with me always.

That Abhishek and Shweta are their father's biggest pride and joy is well known. I am sure if Amitabh were asked what his greatest accomplishments are it would be them, rather than his myriad other triumphs. He holds his children close to his heart with the same bands of steel he did his parents, Dr Harivanshrai and Teji Bachchan. It is no surprise, then, that when I asked Abhishek what the toughest part of being his father's son was, he replied instantly: 'The toughest part would be trying to be as good a son to him as he was to his parents.'

Like I said, an ember from the same fire.

Malavika Sangghvi interviewing Shiv Sena leader Pramod Navalkar.

The first time I met Mumbai's ace photographer Pradeep Chandra was at the iconic rooftop restaurant at the Taj Mahal Apollo Bunder when he had come to photograph me conducting a 'Table For Two' with Shiv Sena leader Pramod Navalkar for *Bombay Times*. I had just returned to Mumbai after almost 10 years, spent in Kolkata and Delhi. Now I was back in the city of my birth, jobless and rudderless. The assignment with Navalkar had come as a lucky break. *Bombay Times*, which had sprung up in my absence, was a popular city supplement, the younger sibling of *The Times of India*. The fact that its chief photographer had come to shoot me with my friend at lunch was definitely a high point of my life at that time. How was anyone—least of all Pradeep Chandra—to know that only a few days later, by a serendipitous assembly of happenchance, I would be reintroduced to him as the editor of *Bombay Times*?

I used to joke at that time that I was an editor on trainer wheels. Newly attempting to learn how to drive, I often wished I could also hang a learner's sign outside my cabin. But, of course, with a daily paper, that was not a luxury I could afford. News came in from all directions at a breakneck speed. Then there were administration responsibilities, HR responsibilities, PR responsibilities and so on. In those days I recall that the chief photographer's (Pradeep Chandra) calm, sanguine and resourceful presence saw me through many a crisis.

'Once you joined and after a few edit meets I discovered that you were very particular about the look of the paper, especially regarding the photography department,' he tells me now, almost 20 years later. 'Slowly Page 3 got a distinctive look and became known as Page 3 ... PEOPLE. Everybody wanted to be featured on the cover or at least on Page 3,' he says.

I remember those days. Long before digital had come to our shores, photographers were shooting on film and even though *The Times of India* had a fully equipped developing studio, the actual retrieval of images from those cool, dark, chemical-reeking rooms was always a cumbersome thing, often fraught with worry and tension. Early on in my editorship I had established that there would always be one iconic and striking image above the fold on the front page across four to five columns, which would be our 'handshake' every morning with our reader—the first thing that would wake him/her up and set the day's tone. We were well into the age of television, where daily visuals of varying attraction jostled for our readers' attention. How would we compete? Our style, look, visual communication would have to be outstanding—starting with the front page daily photograph, which would have to be contextual, riveting, attractive and tell a story of its own. This is where Pradeep Chandra and his department came into play.

'We developed a style of our own and started shooting concept-based pictures,' Chandra recalls. 'Be it MF Husain wearing a three-piece suit in front of a computer, Shobha De with her new book at the swimming pool of The Oberoi with Marine Drive as a backdrop, Harsh Goenka with his collection of paintings, Amrish Puri reading an excerpt from Dharamvir Bharati's book at the National Gallery of Modern Art, they were all memorable,' he says.

And, of course, though Abhishek Bachchan was no more than an industrious school boy in those days, Chandra shot many an iconic portrait of his famous father Amitabh Bachchan for the paper. For the release of his edgy crime cinema noir *Aks*, Chandra had gone the extra mile and asked the film's promoters to organise a huge mirror so he could shoot an artistic 'double image' of the star, which, when it appeared on the front page, was a scene stealer. On another occasion, he saw a boot polish boy working outside Bachchan's Jalsa home and requested the star to pose for a picture with him getting his shoe polished on the street. As the paper grew, so did Chandra's fame and recognition. 'Once when I met Anil Ambani at a Harmony show, he said, "Chandra, when I get the morning papers I keep all of them aside and pick up *BT* to see who you have shot for the day",' Chandra recalls the industrialist saying to him.

As for his desire to dedicate a book to portraits of Abhishek Bachchan, Chandra says he has been shooting him for years, ever since he was a child: 'I remember when he had come to flag off a car rally with his father, as a young boy. He used to accompany his father to the sets often. When I spoke to him about doing this book, he was surprised. "Why me?" he asked. He is well groomed and sophisticated and yet, there is something so earthy and real about him, that he instantly connects with the masses. And even though he has been burdened with unfair expectations, he has come out with flying colours.'

It has been a delight to work with Pradeep Chandra on this book and it has brought back so many wonderful memories of artistic collaborations.

Malavika Sangghvi is a writer, thought-influencer and opinion-maker, who has been described a chronicler of social mores by The New York Times. *She has seen Abhishek Bachchan grow up before her eyes.*

Author's Note

'Why me?' he asked, a bit surprised. And the only response I could offer at that point in time was a smile. Sitting across the table with him and my colleague Amol at the Jalsa office, I sought Abhishek Bachchan's permission to architect a pictorial book on him. I had just gifted him my recent book on MF Husain and a comfortable silence lingered in the air as he went through it. 'Pradeepji, you are writing books on some amazing people, why one on me?' he reiterated. In reply to the rhetoric, I simply sought his permission, which he gracefully gave.

But the question still remains, 'Why Abhishek?' This is a question he asked; a question many ask. A question I choose to answer now, with a counter, 'Why not?' He defines sophistication, success, style and makes us realise how wrong our notions about celebrities and actors are. When it comes to the glamour world we suffer from an audacious myopia, which brutally judges celebrities. We are in the habit of casually drawing conclusions about lives that we read about in glossy magazines and watch through highly-staged truths. But being a photographer/writer has presented me an opportunity to know 'celebrities' as individuals. Each time I click, I unearth and capture a facet of them that draws me to their humble realities. It introduces me to the human side of glamour, where you will find talent—diligent and intense—figuring its way out in this world.

Abhishek is one such talent, an underdog who knows his strengths and lives for himself and his family. Each time I have met him he greets me with a polite 'Namaste'; it is indeed rare for a star kid, educated overseas, to be so simple and down-to-earth. I have caught a glimpse of his simplicity at several occasions. Once he was invited as a chief guest for a football tournament in a school. Before the match began the children requested him to join them on the field. He graciously obliged and played for a while, after which he sat back and watched the game and presented the trophies. Abhishek's love for sports and his sportsman spirit is evident in his conduct. I observed him at a kabbadi tournament where his team was playing. He was a splendid mentor who kept encouraging his team and spearheaded it to victory. Each team member wanted an individual photograph taken with his wife Aishwarya Rai and him; the couple smiled through the entire exercise with amazing warmth. And this was despite the fact that he was to attend a celebration party hosted by Anand Mahindra and then catch an early morning flight to Paris. Such is the energy Abhishek exudes.

In some ways, I find, he is like the legendary Dharmendra. When the latter arrived in Mumbai, Dev Anand, Dilip Kumar and Raj Kapoor were already ruling the film world, followed by Rajendra Kumar, Shammi Kapoor, Rajesh Khanna, the first superstar of Indian cinema and, later, Amitabh Bachchan. But Dharmendra never faltered or faded, he was there, rock steady, giving hits or flops, continuing to have films and fans. Dharmendra never felt insecure being a part of a multi-starrer. He acted with Rajendra Kumar in *Ayee Milan Ki Bela* and *Lalkar*, with Rajesh Khanna in *Dharm Aur Qanoon* and with Amitabh Bachchan in *Ram Balram* and *Sholay*. Similarly, when, in 2000, Abhishek's first film was released, Aamir Khan, Salman Khan and Shah Rukh Khan were ruling the industry; his father had made a comeback that same year with 'Kaun Banega Crorepati'. Abhishek, however, did not shy away or feel insecure. It has been 15 years in films for him, there have been hits and flops and yet, like Dharmendra, he is happy to do films with anyone—be it Shah Rukh Khan in *Happy New Year*; Aamir Khan in *Dhoom 3*; Hrithik Roshan in *Dhoom 2*; Akshay Kumar in *Haan Maine Bhi Pyaar Kiya* or Ajay Devgn in *Bol Bachchan* and *Zameen*. He has also shared screen space with his legendary father in the *Sarkar* series, *Bunty Aur Babli* and *Paa* and is proud to be a part of such movies. This is what made me think of working on this book.

Abhishek intrigued me from the first time I met him and this was way back when he was a kid. He has grown to be an extremely polished and grounded individual. Once, years ago, I was engaged in a heartfelt conversation with Shammi Kapoor at his home. As we exchanged thoughts, he shared this anecdote: 'When I entered the film industry, people used to recognise me as Prithviraj *ka beta*, then they started addressing me as Raj Kapoor's brother and, when I married Geeta Bali, I was viewed as a star's husband. I was living under multiple shadows of people who were worshipped but never did I let myself get lost in those shadows. I worked hard.' Shammi Kapoor rose to success, cutting through severe competition, imprinting in our minds his unique image.

I narrate this anecdote here to draw some parallels. Ever since his launch, Abhishek has lived under a cloud of expectations—'The son of Amitabh and Jaya'; then came, 'The husband of Aishwarya'. It can be daunting to live under such sororities that refuse to acknowledge

The author with Abhishek at the latter's office in Jalsa on a Sunday afternoon. The iconic painting by MF Husain, which the artist had gifted to Amitabh Bachchan, forms the backdrop.

you as a separate individual and attach your being to another's persona. But Abhishek was unperturbed, sure of himself, making decisions that have brought him immense success. He also gracefully accepts failures as his own, admitting that he has learnt a lot from them during the course of his career. What further makes him a person with immense depth is his respect for women, be it his mother, wife, colleague or a tribal woman in Odisha, where he has travelled to as a part of the End 7 Campaign, The Global Network for Neglected Tropical Diseases in India, of which he is an ambassador.

Despite tough competition, Abhishek has carved a niche in an industry that is supposedly claimed to be ruled by the Khans. Movies such as *Guru, Yuva, Sarkar, Dum Maaro Dum* and *Dhoom* reflect his versatility. If we were to select just one film of his, however, I feel he has given a performance of a lifetime in *Guru*. His intensity, character adaptation and diligence are unmatched.

There are many sides to him, besides acting. Abhishek is a sports lover who has chosen to support kabbadi and football. His business acumen is commendable. And his ability to blend style with simplicity is fascinating. He is one of the few actors who donned three-piece suits at a very young age. He has a knack for fashion and carries trends with great panache. Abhishek has a shoe fetish, so much so that he gets shoes custom-made. Recently, while travelling with him, I noticed him wearing shoes that had his initial 'A' inscribed on them.

The urge to know more about a person like him propelled me to write this book. But, along with me, my camera, too, is equally drawn to Abhishek. He is an interesting subject because he displays a plethora of emotions without any hesitation. I have been clicking him since he was a kid. I vividly remember when, in the 1970s, Amitabh was shooting at the swimming

Abhishek going through the images that had been shortlisted for this book by the author.

pool in Mumbai's Holiday Inn for *Amar Akbar Anthony* and, during the break, he was sitting with both his kids comfortably perched on his lap. This was a time when he was off the press but he still allowed me to take some photographs. After many clicks, he humbly said, 'Bus, *kitni* photo *lehnge aap*?' [Stop, how many photographs are you going to take?]. Another memory I have of clicking Abhishek was when he came to a film muhurat sitting on his father's shoulder. Unfortunately the picture belonged to the publication I was taking photographs for and thus I do not have the negatives of this delightful image.

I also recollect the time when Abhishek had come to flag-off a car rally with his father and Dilip Kumar. I had no clue that I would end up doing a book on him and that, too, after completing *AB, The Legend: A Photographer's Tribute* on his father. Nonetheless I made it a point to click him at every possible opportunity, right from his debut in *Refugee* to *Delhi-6*. My first shoot of Abhishek as an actor was on the sets of *Refugee* when I was assisting JP Singhal, a renowned painter and photographer. Another earlier, memorable photograph is that of Abhishek kissing his mother after receiving the Filmfare award. I also have some amazing black-and-white photographs of his first press conference hosted at Palm Hotel, Juhu. During the shoot of *Dhaai Akshar Prem Ke*, I was given the opportunity of shooting him for two days, and he was supportive and friendly.

During the shooting of *Delhi-6*, he was required to report at the sets at Madh Island early in the morning. It surprised me to see that he chose to travel by ferry, which he boarded at Versova, interacting with the other passengers. As I joined him, he simply said, 'It saves so much time'. Abhishek always goes out of the way to put a photographer at ease. During the shooting of *Shararat* at Worli, he invited me to his vanity van and asked what kind of pictures I had in mind. He heard me out patiently so that he could help me get my shots in the best possible way.

Facing page: Abhishek caught unawares on camera.

Left: Chief Guest Amitabh Bachchan and Pradeep Chandra with guests at an exhibition of photographs and artworks that the author had held in celebration of Amitabh's 61st birthday.

He is jovial and friendly towards all with a sense of humour that is rather infectious. Once when he landed on the sets of *Delhi-6*, he saw 15 cameras mounted all across and he promptly asked, '*Aur koi* cameras *bache nahi the kya?*' [There were no more cameras left?]. Often when he would sit for lunch he would say, '*Dekho bhai aaj Bahurani ne kya bheja hai*' [Let's see what Bahurani has sent]. I suppose he was referring to Aishwarya. He is just like his father when it comes to punctuality. He is a photographer's delight and is extremely co-operative. Years ago I was doing a special shoot of Akshay Kumar and Karisma Kapoor for *Bombay Times* at the Filmalaya Studio when Abhishek casually walked towards me, removed the spare camera hanging on my neck and said, 'At times even you should be photographed' and he took a whole roll of my pictures. I found this to be a really sweet gesture.

It is for the joy of clicking and knowing him that I write this book, which contains a series of unseen and exclusive pictures and drawings of the actor. I hope it acts as a window and shows the reader the Abhishek I know. For me this book is all the more special as I have shot so many pictures of his grandfather Dr Harivanshrai Bachchan during my *Saptahik Hindustan* days in Delhi and then, later, of his father Amitabh Bachchan, whose photographs I have been taking for several decades. I even celebrated Amitabh's 61st birthday with a series of artworks and photographs at the JW Marriott hotel, which he was gracious enough to inaugurate. Then came Abhishek's debut in *Refugee* and the cycle moves on.

The only fear I have is that I will wake up one day and nobody will allow me to do films. This is a fear every actor has.

INTRODUCTION

Honest words, from someone whose name means 'bold'. According to journalist Bhuvendra Tyagi, the word 'Abhishek' figured first in the Rig Veda. It was later spotted in the Upanishads, Ramayan and the Gita as well as in several other Sanskrit epics. From there it travelled to Hindi, where it is identified with the gods; the anointment on the forehead is called Abhishek. Tyagi elaborates:

> It contains two components: *abhi* and *shek*. *Abhi* means towards information, higher, new; *shek* has been derived from *sek*, which means go, move. Hence a combination of *abhi* and *sek* implies moving towards higher goals and acquiring new knowledge. Swami Vivekananda used it in the sense of being bold; for him, the basic meaning of the word is boldness.

Multiple adjectives can be used to define Abhishek Bachchan; some of them conflicting. Sincere and suave; intense and intelligent, he is considered by many as the cool 'hot guy' of Hindi cinema. Rugged masculine looks, style and charm are part of the persona of a star, an actor, a celebrity. Yet he is a man of many milestones, in areas as diverse as movies, sports and business. An actor, producer, playback singer and television host, Abhishek has excelled in his many roles. His sincerity towards life and his profession is evident. His parents, Amitabh Bachchan and Jaya Bhaduri, ruled Indian cinema, his father is hailed as a living legend, but what he inherited from them was values, not vanity. Being a Bachchan and especially the son of Amitabh comes with an overwhelming burden of expectations and attention, but he has managed to deal with it in a manner that appears effortless.

Facing page: The legendary actors, power couple Jaya and Amitabh Bachchan.

Left: Being interviewed on television.

Abhishek's rugged looks and brooding presence did not go unnoticed by the critics.

'He has a brooding on-screen image which is quite different from the complete prankster he is in real life. I can see now why he makes girls go weak in the knees,' wrote Kaveree Bamzai, Executive Editor, *India Today* (August 2005). 'What sets Abhishek apart is his blend of western sophistication and home-grown values. He is, as one director says, "the first hip hop Hindi film star".'

This tag and his success have, however, not been easy to achieve. Abhishek's debut film, *Refugee* (2000), earned little praise and was followed by a string of commercially unsuccessful films. It was four years later that his role in *Yuva* was critically acclaimed. The action thriller *Dhoom* was also released in 2004. It was a box office hit and the first part of the popular *Dhoom* series. Several hit movies followed: *Bunty Aur Babli, Sarkar, Kabhi Alvida Naa Kehna, Guru, Dhoom 2, Dostana, Paa, Bol Bachchan, Dhoom 3* and the latest *Happy New Year*. Abhishek has also received several accolades in recognition of his work, including the Filmfare Award, the National Award for producing *Paa* and the Yash Bharti award, Uttar Pradesh's highest cultural honour.

As an actor, one of the most striking aspects about him is his versatility; from an action hero, a romantic rogue, a serious character, to a comic one—he has played it all with confidence. Backing his talent is his capacity for hard work. In February 2009, he travelled seven cities for the promotion of *Delhi-6* in 12 hours. This feat made him the first Indian film star to be included in the Guinness Book of World Records. Yet another role that he has assumed with success is that of a producer, the first movie he produced was *Paa*. In an interview with *The Times of India* he shared his experience:

With Sonam Kapoor during the shooting of Delhi-6, *directed by Rakeysh Omprakash Mehra.*

> I hate producing films. It's just that I got lucky [with *Paa*]. But I hate it. During *Paa*, I had a very difficult time because the producer in me came in the way of the actor in me. I would be more comfortable in producing a film without acting in it. If I have to produce a film in which I am acting, that would need a lot of preparation and organisation from my part.

But he then went on, in typical Bachchan style, to produce another film—R Balki's *Shamitabh*, which starred Amitabh Bachchan and Dhanush. This, he observed, proved to be a more enjoyable experience but that did not deter him from confessing that production is a difficult and thankless job.

Abhishek's biggest critic is his own father who has, on every occasion, asked him to push the envelope. Amitabh's praises have always been measured, until the day he saw his son's work in *Guru*: 'Abhishek is phenomenal. I have held myself back on so many occasions from commenting on my son's work, but this time I shall not. To hell with niceties and restraint. Abhishek is incredible.'

Amitabh loves it when he sees a crowd of fans outside his house waiting not only for him but his son:

> The well-wishers surge in numbers … they are excited and loud in their love … the gates, unable to contain their enthusiasm, are not enough to hold them at a distance … there is a special attraction today—Abhishek aka Nandu Bhide from *HNY* [*Happy New Year*]. Feel a sense of pride to see him thus … not new to it, but still new is never enough when children are concerned.

Abhishek's acting skills in Guru *(left) and the recent* Happy New Year *(right) have won him much appreciation.*

Dr Deepak Chaturvedi, co-Founder and Medical Director, Antiaging Medicine and Research (AMAR), is an avid fan who finds Abhishek to be a brilliant actor with a huge potential:

> With all due respect to the senior Bachchan, I unabashedly state that Abhishek is at par with him as an actor. I was bowled over by Abhishek and his work in the *Sarkar* series. Every actor displays some degree of nervousness while sharing screen space with the legendary senior Bachchan, Abhishek stood out; he appeared confident and in control. That brings me to another aspect I admire about Abhishek—his comfort in sharing screen space with every star of the industry, including the three Khans. The media has often been over-critical about him, but, in my view, as an actor he has proved himself with each passing movie right from *Refugee* to *Happy New Year*. He is a brand for the *Dhoom* series. We have witnessed him play many characters, intense and comic. At six feet three inches, with dashing stubble, flawless diction and a good sense of music, Abhishek has all the ingredients of a star, which he is.

It was on the sets of *Guru* that the love between Abhishek and Aishwarya grew; Abhishek proposed to her at its premiere and they became Bollywood's power couple. *Time* magazine has named the three Bachchans—Amitabh, Abhishek and Aishwarya Rai—on its list of most influential Indians.

Facing page: Taking confident strides in Delhi-6.

Right: Aishwarya's and Abhishek's love story blossomed during the shooting of Guru.

Abhishek has also endorsed many brands such as LG Home Appliances, American Express Platinum Club, Videocon DTH, Motorola Mobiles, Ford Fiesta and Idea Mobiles. His portrayal of 'Sirji' in the Idea commercial has been widely appreciated. He is doing the Prestige home appliances advertisement with Aishwarya.

Sport is another passion for Abhishek who has been endorsing and promoting kabbadi and soccer in India. His favourite sport continues to be basketball; he is the first Indian who participated in the National Basketball Association (NBA) all-star celebrity game. He is slowly developing into a sports entrepreneur with his Pro Kabaddi League (PKL) team, Jaipur Pink Panthers and Indian Super League (ISL) franchise.

The actor has a philanthropic side to him and has supported many causes, including the END7 campaign for women in Odisha (of which he is the ambassador); Ride for Safety with the Mumbai police and Plan India, which works for the upliftment of deprived children.

Above: Abhishek's 'Sirji' in the Idea commercial got him a lot of recognition.

Facing page: With Aamir Khan and his daughter, Ira, at a football match.

SKINS
adidas
adidas

Let us come together
and make FILARIA free society.
CASA
Member of
actalliance
GLOBAL NETWORK
IMA WorldHealth
We are thankful to the Health & Family Welfare Dept.
Govt. of Odisha for their co-operation

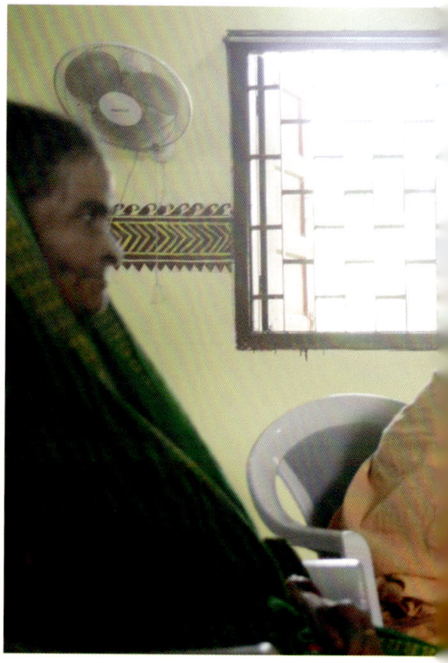

As ambassador of the the END7 campaign for women in Odisha, Abhishek interacting with filaria patients and doctors.

Facing page: Catching up on his sleep during a flight.

Above: On his way to Odisha.

He has an inherent sense of style, probably inherited from his father. In 2012, *GQ* magazine brought out its third edition of the 50 most stylish and best dressed men in India; Abhishek featured in this list. Noted Fulvia Visconti Ferragamo: 'Abhishek Bachchan can claim to be a style icon. His frame and friendly demeanour help him carry off most looks, whether formal or casual. His clothes, mostly black or white, reflect class and good taste.' The next year, he won the Style Icon of the Country Award in New Delhi.

Abhishek is now preparing for three sequels—*Dostana 2*, *Hera Pheri 3* and *Housefull 3*. He also celebrated his 39th birthday in February 2015, which was highlighted in Amitabh's nostalgic blog post: 'The birthday has been brought in and Abhishek is another year older, 39 years ... strange but he was born just the other day ... and the euphoria and the champagne opening at the Breach Candy Hospital, the traditional cigar smoked, general joy and celebration.'

And, as he now plays one of his most significant real-life roles—that of father to Aaradhya (born in November 2011)—Abhishek says, with all sincerity: 'By the

A style icon, Abhishek at designer Manish Malhotra's fashion show.

Celebrating the Maharashtrian New Year, Gudi Padwa, with wife Aishwarya.

grace of God, my parents were fantastic. We were a very normal family, and we have had a very middle-class Indian upbringing. We were never made to realise who we were or that my father and mother were huge stars—it was a very normal house, and I'd like my daughter to have the same thing.'

I am told, I was 3.7 kg, 19.5 inches tall and the name that was entered immediately in the hospital register was 'Baba Bachchan'.

STARTING YOUNG

This day (5 February 1976) marked the beginning of a childhood that was magical, a chapter full of love and care, propped with ponies, teddies and plays. While his famous father was brought home, with little fanfare, in a *tonga* (carriage) in Allahabad, Abhishek arrived in a Mercedes in Mumbai. His early years were a blend of being good and being bratty. The first word he learnt to speak was 'Pa'; he was merely seven months old then. He recollects:

> Ma and Pa would constantly emphasise that we should not look scruffy and unkempt. I would be dressed in shorts, black shoes with white socks pulled right up to my knee. I must have looked like an extraterrestrial species but my parents must have believed that I looked smart. When I was three, we were in New York and I was made to wear a three-piece suit with a clip-on tie. Shwetdi and I would be instructed repeatedly to clean the room, comb our hair and generally do the right thing. We had nannies to do our work but were taught not to become dependent on household help.

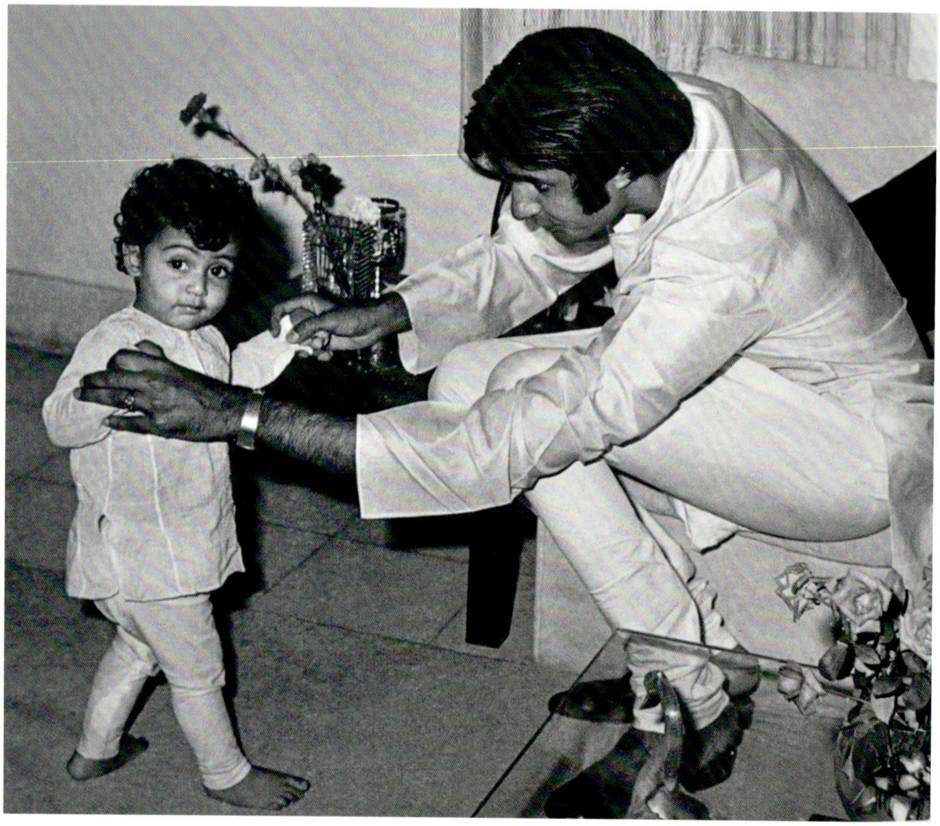

An early photograph of Abhishek where his father helps him to take tentative steps.

Prateeksha (left), where Abhishek spent his childhood years and Jalsa, the residence of the Bachchans.

An important part of Abhishek's growing up years was Prateeksha, where the Bachchans lived before shifting to their present residence, Jalsa. He vividly remembers a gulmohar sapling that was planted by his father right in the middle of the garden when he was barely three months old. The garden's periphery had palm trees, a plantain tree and flower bushes, there was also a Christmas tree. He would climb the walls and water pump cabins and indulge in all kinds of theatrics in the garden.

Jaya and Amitabh look on as Abhishek gets his hair cut.

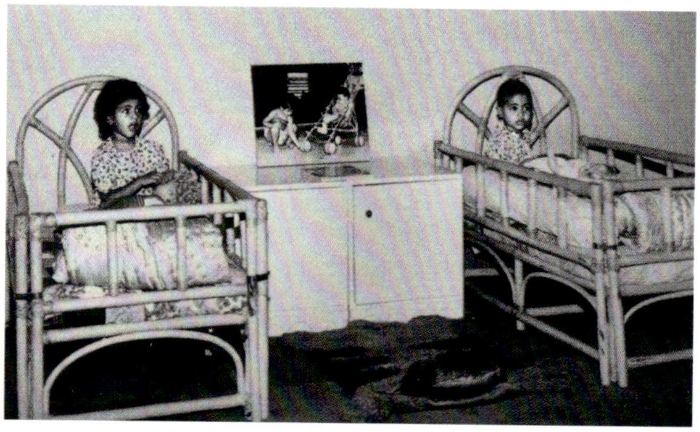

Amitabh poses with his young son (left) and a view of the nursery of Abhishek and his sister Shweta (right).

Abhishek and his sister Shweta's nursery was a dreamland for kids. It had two cane beds, a small play area sprinkled with a huge pile of soft toys, glowing green lamps and a teddy bear, fondly called 'John'. John was Abhishek's favourite; it even travelled with him to London, occupying an entire seat on the airplane. At times, Abhishek used to sit on John's lap. (According to him, John is still stuffed and alive in their Delhi home, Sopan.) The nursery connected straight into their parents' room, which had slanted ceilings, black beams, a dark wooden floor and a bed equivalent to the size of a playground. The vastness of the bed used to make Abhishek turn crazy and he enjoyed somersaulting on it every morning. His first nanny, Umadevi from Darjeeling, would go insane trying to control him. Shweta was his partner in crime. 'Shweta and I—our relationship was not that of a sister and brother, but of two children bonded together in a world run by adults,' he remembers. 'I would call her Shwetdi because Shweta didi was too cumbersome. Now everyone, including our parents, call her Shwetdi.'

Shweta was surrounded by her dolls and tea sets; Abhishek would be playing with his imaginary goblins and ogres. The two also had their own little games and acts: 'I would tie her to a tree, playing the roles of her abductor as well as her saviour. Then we had the dangerous games, where, for example, she would be holding a bunch of balloons and I would be aiming at them with an air rifle, feeling very much like William Tell.' The siblings had their share of fights as well, one of which left Shweta tied to a pole for several hours. Abhishek and Shweta were playing badminton, on losing she refused to pick up the shuttlecock. Abhishek promptly tied her to a pole and left her there. She hollered for as long as four hours.

Abhishek and Shweta share a loving moment with their father.

Amitabh's parents, Harivanshrai Bachchan (left) and Teji Bachchan (right) played a significant role in Abhishek's growing up years.

The two had a gang of their own, comprising their cousins Nilima, Namrata, Naina and Bhimkarma. They were inseparable and only went to their respective homes to sleep:

> My cousins, Shwetdi and I were a team. We had even formed a rock band called Bloodsuckers, all for our private amusement, of course. I would wear these spaced-out goggles with winking lights. We had seen this movie called *Breakin'*, we were into copying breakdance steps. Ma and Pa would suffer through our disco performances, smiling benignly. Pa, I remember, had brought us the audio and videotapes of Michael Jackson's *Thriller*. So we tried our best to copy Jackson too.

Abhishek went to many schools and yet it appears he adapted to the environment in each quite easily. His school days, where he pursued his interests such as acting and sports, were full of fun and friends. From Bombay Scottish to Switzerland, the journey has been exciting. Formal education was of prime importance at the Bachchan house and thus Abhishek was sent to the Montessori play school, Tiny Tots and then Miniland when he was barely out of his diapers. Bombay Scottish was his first school and he still meets his carpool friends—Aditya and Uday (Yash Chopra's sons), Goldie and Nanu (producer Ramesh Behl's children), Hrithik and Sunaina (Rakesh Roshan's children), Jatin (actor Sujit Kumar's son), Amit and Sumit (sons of director Prakash Mehra) and Vinay (who works for Bacardi). Karan Johar, who lived at Malabar Hill then, would see Abhishek and Shweta occasionally,

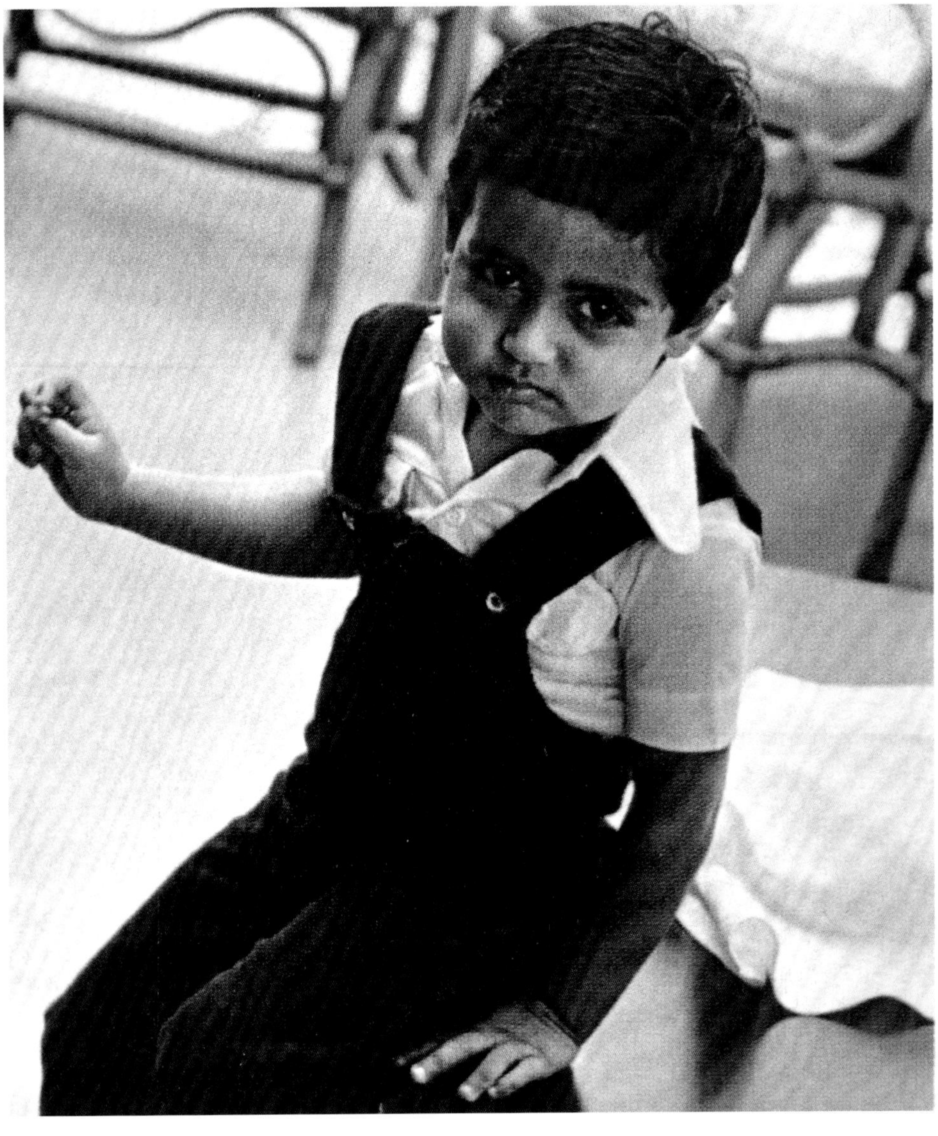

According to Abhishek, his parents were very particular about the fact that he and his sister, even as children, should not look scruffy.

usually at their joint birthday party. Karan reminisces, 'We would have these dancing competitions in which Adi [Aditya] invariably came first. Amit uncle was the judge.' They still meet often; Johar recalls the coffee he, Aditya and Abhishek had recently: 'There we were, the three idiots who would go to fancy dress parties together, being so comfortable in the same space.' Apart from his school gang, Abhishek and Rohan Gavaskar are close friends; they play scrabble whenever they meet.

From Bombay Scottish, Abhishek was shifted to Jamnabai School (1983), since it was closer to their home. He studied there for about two years. According to his then teacher Evan Fernandes, 'Abhishek was a shy, obedient, kind and loving kid who made friends easily. He was a fairly good student and didn't throw his weight around. He loved playing sports and took part in a lot of sports activities such as football, basketball, handball and so on.' For Abhishek, this change of school did not make much of a difference because he is quick to adapt, just like his father. Apart from this trait, Amitabh and Abhishek share a common affliction—reverse vertigo: 'We want to jump off whenever we look down from a height even if it is just from a 30 metre-high cliff. I would vault down the stairs and leap off parapets and, since I was accident-prone, Pa would be there cleaning my wounds ever so clinically.'

Abhishek studied at Jamnabai School in Mumbai.

*The Bachchan family—
Abhishek recalls
having a magical
childhood, a chapter
full of love and care.*

Facing page: His fascination for the camera continues.

Left: Abhishek confesses to being a mischievous kid, prone to throwing tantrums.

Abhishek, post the age of three, was very mischievous:

> I was a real Tasmanian devil always, breaking something or injuring myself. Till I was three I was this nice ideal baby but after that I must have been making up for lost time. Maybe they dropped me on my head or something because I had turned into a monster of mischief. I was known for throwing tantrums, the most irritating one being at the Singapore airport when I had insisted on buying some toy or the other from the duty-free shop. My parents left me sitting on the floor, saying, 'Okay you stay here, we are leaving'. In a flash I was running after them, crying that it was mean of them to abandon me.

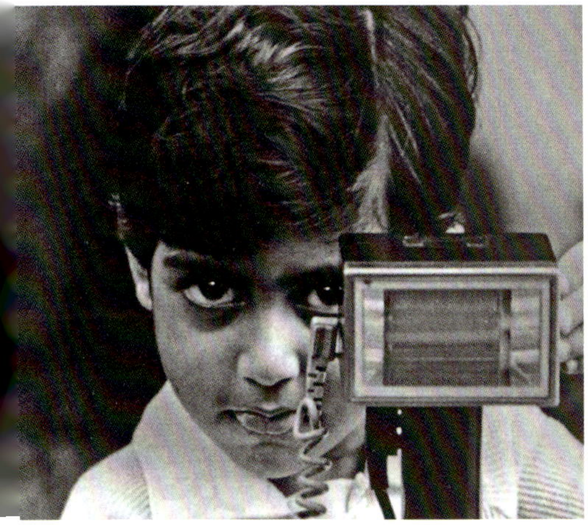

There has always been a huge emphasis on family togetherness among the Bachchans.

The next move happened when Amitabh decided to join politics and they had to shift base to Delhi. Abhishek was really happy there. He and Shweta were admitted to Modern School. Says Richa Mudgal, Abhishek's class teacher:

> Before Abhishek and his sister joined the school, his grandparents [Dr Harivanshrai and Teji Bachchan] came to survey the school and were particularly pleased when they saw a Hindi poem written on the blackboard in one of the classrooms. Being a tall kid, he was usually made to occupy the last bench in the class! The kids had joined the school a month later after the school reopened. I gave him a classmate's book to enable him catch up on all the lost work. After a few days, he brought the book back and gave his book for correction too. I was surprised to see the entire work written beautifully and neatly and wondered if he had written it. He was frank enough to admit that his dad Amitabh had copied all the notes for him. I was pleasantly surprised to see the involvement of the family to ensure that their kids were always up to the mark.

Abhishek has his own special memories of schooling in Delhi:

> Shwetdi and I would return from Modern School at 1 pm. We were made to nap for an hour after lunch. By then I had a room of my own, even equipped with Roman rings. My grandparents were in Delhi, Chacha [Ajitabh Bachchan] and my cousins were at a Mehrauli farmhouse. Everything seemed to be more spacious and comfortable to a child who did not realise the extent of turmoil that his father was going through in politics.

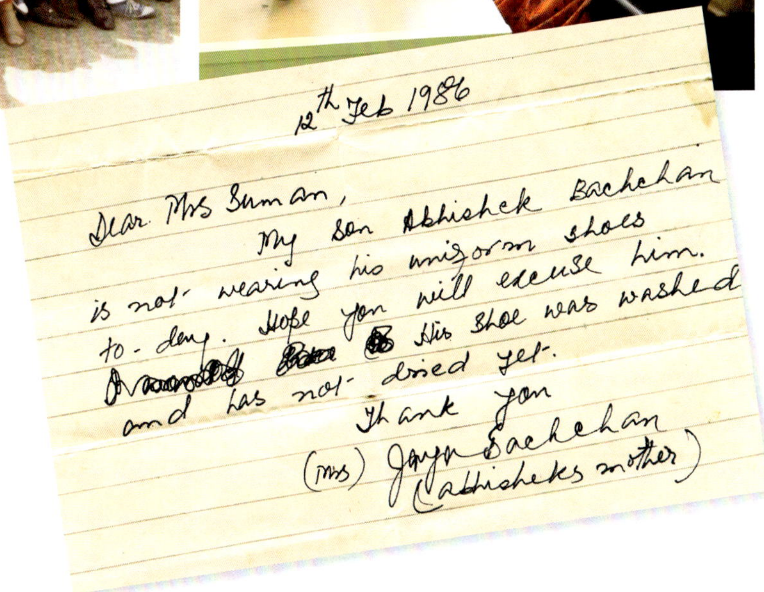

12th Feb 1986

Dear Mrs Suman,
My son Abhishek Bachchan is not wearing his uniform shoes to-day. Hope you will excuse him. His shoe was washed and has not dried yet.
Thank you
(Mrs) Jaya Bachchan
(Abhisheks mother)

Clockwise from bottom right: Note sent by Jaya Bachchan to Abhishek's teacher; Ajitabh, Ramola and Jaya Bachchan at a function held at Modern School, New Delhi; Abhishek's teachers at Modern School—Suman Malasi, Richa Mudgal and Bharti Anand.

On the academic front, Abhishek admits he was an average student. His Hindi teacher at Modern School, Bharti Anand, observes that his Hindi had a Bombay dialect to it: 'Once while correcting his examination paper, I wondered whether to deduct his marks over the purity of the language and then decided otherwise as I felt he had understood the subject matter well and the answers were accurate.' His father would take an active interest in his studies and help him in mathematics, tables and logarithms. 'He would instruct me on how to rewrite my English essays when I had made a mess of them, which was very often,' shares Abhishek. 'Pa made sure that my handwriting improved. He is ambidextrous: he writes with his right hand but eats and plays sports with his left hand. I am the opposite: I write with my left hand, like Chacha, who is also left-handed.' His sports teacher Suman Malasi recollects, 'Once he came wearing the wrong shoes to school and I punished him. The next day he still came without the sports shoes but with a letter from his mother, Jayaji, saying that the shoes had been washed and were wet, so please excuse him.'

Amitabh and Abhishek seen with legendary Hindi film producer and director Prakash Mehra at Shanmukhananda hall, Mumbai.

Post-Delhi came something that Abhishek dreaded—the day he would have to live without his parents. He was about nine or 10 then, being sent off to a school in Switzerland. The 10 km drive up to the school seemed like eternity: 'I was all choked up inside, looking at my parents with accusing eyes as if to ask, "How can you do this to me?" I was very scared, but the minute I set foot on the campus, all my fears vanished. I fitted in with the rest of the kids.' The siblings learnt French there, but whenever they went back home for vacation, which was every three months, Amitabh would make it a point that they spoke in chaste Hindi.

Abhishek's parents mean the world to him: 'The door would be left ajar always. They had this fetish about closed doors. Both Ma and Pa would never shut themselves away from Shweta and me.' There was a huge emphasis on family togetherness, Sunday being a sacrosanct day for the adults as well as kids. These memories remain:

> Pa loved the family huddling together on that big bed in Prateeksha. Ma would sing lullabies, which Shwetdi now sings to her children. When we had dozed off, Pa would pick us up and tuck us into our beds. He would pat our heads, play with our hair gently. He still does that whenever he chooses to put me to bed, especially if I am unwell or restless. At the age of nine of 10, I would pretend to be asleep. I wanted him to pick me up in his arms, but obviously, I had become too heavy. I was always woken up after that, there was no more lifting of the baby in the arms.

Yet another ritual that Amitabh loved was hosting elaborate birthday parties for both the kids. On his first birthday, Abhishek was decked up in a sherwani and, when he turned seven, he was gifted a pony. Sharing yet another ritual the father and son followed, Abhishek says, 'Pa would bathe me himself, right till I was 11 years old. He would apply mustard oil on my body, coconut oil in my hair and then splash lukewarm water all over me from a brass *lota* [round water pot], the way they do in Allahabad.'

Abhishek with sister Shweta.

The attachment Abhishek has for his father runs deep, as is evident from this anecdote: One day, Abhishek saw his father's movie *Barsaat Ki Ek Raat* and was simply appalled when Amjad Khan started beating Amitabh. He howled on witnessing the scene. Some days later, Abhishek saw his father shooting with Amjad who, incidentally, used to call Amitabh 'Shorty'. Abhishek ran towards Amjad and started punching him because he was terribly upset with him. Both Amitabh and Amjad had a hearty laugh at this incident.

As a child, the biggest event in his life would be his father returning home at the end of the day: 'I would keep staring at the door and the vacant space beyond it till he walked in dramatically. On sighting him, I would jump on his back and hold him tight right till the time I became heavier, taller and a pain in the neck.' He goes on to narrate:

> In 1982, when I was six, Pa was carried into our suite at the West End Hotel in Bangalore [now Bengaluru]. I bounded towards him happily, eager to jump on his back, not realising that he had been grievously injured [he had a near fatal accident during the shooting of *Coolie*]. That was the first and last time he pushed me away from him. I was so upset about the snub that I immediately went into a big sulk. All four of us in the family are huge sulk masters. Ma and I sulk for an hour or two but Pa's and Shwetdi's sulks can last for a month.

Abhishek with Jaya and Shweta, who have always been very supportive towards him.

The door was left ajar and Abhishek could see his father moaning in excruciating pain. As he was sulking, he ignored his father, concentrating, instead, on his Pac-Man video game. The next morning, he and his sister were packed off to Mumbai; the first time they were flying alone. He recalls going to the Breach Candy Hospital every day to see his father, who was in the intensive care unit (ICU). In an interview with *India Today*, he noted that it was like one big game: 'Whenever we walked into the ICU, my dad would point at all the bottles and drips and say, "Look I've got kites for you." We were preoccupied with wearing masks and playing the doctor. It wasn't a time of sorrow or distress.'

The nurses used to give the two children masks so that they could play doctor-doctor in the lounge outside. While his parents tried to make this phase as mellow as possible for the children, there were times when the dark side of reality would reach him. Once, when he was playing in the school backyard during recess, a kid came up to him and asked, 'Your father is going to die, isn't he?' The question had a tremendous impact on Abhishek, he blanked out and at night he suffered from a severe asthmatic attack:

> Ma was going through hell, dealing with two guys, one at hospital and the other at home. The next day I was allowed to miss school, which was fantastic for a kid. I remember being propped up in bed, watching *Star Wars* on video and crunching on a chocolate-wafer slab. I may have been six, but children at that age are aware that there is something called death. I was petrified for Pa, but tried not to show it.

Attending a function with Amitabh and Shweta.

> I would pray every night, begging for his recovery, at the same time sneaking in a request for a new toy or a pencil set.

The day Amitabh came out of the hospital from Room No. 306, hair cropped, walking with a stick, Abhishek, who reached up to his knees, clutched his father's finger tightly and tried to steer him through the massive crowd that had gathered in the hospital's compound. It was his little way of protecting his dad, a habit which he still has of clutching on to his father's finger in a crowd.

The relationship that Abhishek shares with his father is that of a friend: 'It was Dada [his paternal grandfather] who said that a son ceases to be a son the day he can fit into his father's shoes. We both wear size 10 and I fitted into Pa's shoes at the age of 14.' The buddy factor runs back that long. They watch soccer matches together and, since the time he was a kid, Amitabh would treat him like an equal, like the man of the house:

> When he would leave for an out-of-town schedule, Pa would request me to look after my Ma and sister. Whenever we would be caught in a crowd, his index finger would drop right before my eyes and I would clutch at it. Ma and Shwetdi would be there, trailing behind us and he would say, while holding my hand, 'Come, let's look after the women'. He would encourage me, even as a kid, to take charge of situations.

In his eyes, 'Pa' was a Superman. On one of his birthdays, Abhishek recollects, both Ajitabh and his father had dressed up in Superman costumes:

> I would insist that my Pa is the strongest father of them all. I remember a holiday in Kashmir when my friend, Chirag Doshi, had picked up an argument saying that his father is stronger than mine. I retaliated by yelling at the top of my voice that my Pa could bash up 50 men at a time. Today, Chirag and I rib each other about how crazy we were.

Abhishek used to dream about his father when he was away and hoped to grow up to be just like him. He wished he would have his father's height, his luxuriant hair and baritone voice. 'I have his height today. I am half-an-inch taller, but in other respects, of course, I am nowhere near him,' he says. Abhishek never felt his father's absence because they kept in touch through letters, though it was often difficult for Abhishek to keep pace with the correspondence. When he went on his first date in Switzerland, he was barely 12; the first one to know about this was his father. Abhishek had written telling him that he liked a girl,

Celebrating Abhishek's birthday. Seen with the children are Ajitabh and Amitabh.

to which Amitabh wrote back that we was happy to know that. 'Whenever we talked to each other about delicate matters, it has always been via letters. Perhaps we express ourselves better on paper since my Dada was a writer and my Nana [his maternal grandfather], a journalist,' notes Abhishek. He recollects the first intense father-son talk they had:

> I had just finished school in the summer of 1994. We were at the crater island town of Santorini in Greece. Pa asked the rest of the family to stay at the hotel while he took me out for lunch at a restaurant. The sunlight was dazzling white; the ocean was a translucent blue. For more than four hours, he talked to me about what he expected of me and I expressed my feelings about what I wanted to do. The nub of the talk was that we were both in the same team—what should our game plan for the future be? The idea of ABCL [Amitabh Bachchan Corporation Ltd] was formulating in his mind then, he made me privy to his plans. For the first time Pa had accepted me as a man, he wanted me to take care of things when he could not.

Being Amitabh's best friend, he has been the more pampered child of the two: 'I am a baby who is still in the house and I use that to arm-twist my parents whenever the need arises.' But there are limits to the pampering; there are certain things even his best buddy cannot tolerate. The most stringent punishment Abhishek has received from his father was to stand in a corner by the window silently for 15 minutes. There is yet another incident that Abhishek has mentioned in the pictorial biography, *To Be or Not to Be*, 'At Disneyland in Orlando, I had lied to Pa about finishing a pineapple flavour ice cream which I detested. He was furious that I had lied, but cooled down the next day and treated me to all the Disneyland joy rides which had been denied to me.'

All things considered, Abhishek readily confesses he is a mama's boy: 'Ma was the more forceful disciplinarian of the two. As a kid, I would, on occasion, be given a tight slap by her but she would be sorry the next minute and cuddle me as if she had been in the wrong.' Jaya's 'AB baby' has been wrapped around her little finger often. She once said, 'I come from a home where my mother was always around. Just her presence gave me a lot of strength. I became the person I am because of her.' Jaya never considered breaking away from her professional life as a sacrifice: 'I don't think I am an extraordinary mother. I come from a decent middle-class family. I have just behaved normally with my children.' Abhishek said in an interview, 'One day Shwetdi and I were watching *Mili.* My sister was crying and I was smiling. My mom walked in, saw that she was crying and slapped me, thinking that I had done something to make her cry! But the next minute she was guilty and hugging me too.'

Acting and sports form two integral parts of Abhishek's life. His first play was staged at Mumbai's Shanmukhananda hall when he was in school. He enacted the role of a singing daisy; both his parents were part of the audience. Abhishek then got a bigger part in a Jamnabai School play, where he played the lead role of the Big Bear Red Indian chief in the operetta, *At the End of the Warpath.* Amitabh had attended the performance and had photographed all the kids using a video camera. At AEGON College in Villars, Switzerland, he acted in stage plays, *Oh! What a Lovely War, The Importance of Being Earnest* and *The Pirates of Penance.* Abhishek had some disagreements with the director during *The Pirates of Penance*; to clarify his point and seek advice he promptly wrote to his father who replied saying that, like movies, theatre is a director's medium. Once the actor is on stage emoting, only then can he be in charge of his performance. Abhishek was to take it from there. Amitabh, however, made it a point to attend this play. 'I expected him to gush that I was brilliant. He didn't. He said that I was good, but far too jovial and vociferous when the performance could have been more understated,' recollects Abhishek. 'Now that was exactly my point of difference with the director. The first bit of criticism from Pa made it clear that he would always be a hard taskmaster.'

He was selected for the school's senior basketball team at Aegon. Unfortunately, a day before the match, Abhishek injured his left leg during practice and was unable to participate. He was devastated. Knowing the situation, his father called immediately but Abhishek was too upset to talk. The next day his school team entered the stadium with Abhishek hobbling behind them on crutches. Among the supporters he spotted his father who had taken the first flight to Switzerland to be with him. Abhishek also used to play kabbadi during his student days in Delhi.

As a child he had learnt sarod from the maestro Ustad Amjad Ali Khan who said in an interview to *Hindustan Times* that Abhishek learnt how to play the instrument with his sons, Amaan and Aaryan Ali Khan: 'He was 10 then and he is still very passionate about it. I have great love, admiration and fondness for the Bachchan family.' Abhishek also learnt driving that year. After much

Jaya and Shweta–the two ladies in young Abhishek's life.

persuasion and howling on his part, his father had allowed him to take the wheel at Ranthambore National Park. In a way, Abhishek's childhood was like a joy ride in itself. He had it all—doting parents, a supportive sibling, the madness of friends and a sense of passion.

When I was a kid, I wanted to be everything. I saw a movie; I wanted to be an astronaut; I wanted to be like Gordon Gekko; I wanted to be a fireman or a race car driver. Then I realised, there is a common link: You're seeing it through the movies. Be an actor; you can be all of them.

BEING AN ACTOR

Acting was not just about genes for Abhishek Bachchan, it was a conscious choice. He always wanted to be an actor; it was a passion that grew owing to the environment he lived in. Visiting and hanging around at his father's film sets and being groomed by his school drama coach, Desmond Hann, were just part of his growing up years. But Amitabh wanted him to get a formal education and thus Abhishek was enrolled into Boston University. He returned to Mumbai to help with Shweta's wedding preparations for which he took a semester off and then never went back. He decided to quit Boston University and pursue acting; a decision his father supported. Thus began what has turned out to be a thrilling saga for the young Bachchan.

With JP Dutta who launched him in Refugee.

Even though the myth still prevails that it is easy for star kids to enter Bollywood and make it big, the truth is far more complex. A young lad, ambitious and nervous, was burdened with the overpowering expectation of filling his 'larger than life' father's shoes. Being Amitabh Bachchan's son and an actor meant you had to shine; being average was not an option. It was not easy to begin with. He remembers calling directors and producers, seeking work and their support. 'No one was rude, I think they had too much respect for my father', but no one wanted to take the risk or responsibility of launching him. The 20-year-old aspirant attended some acting workshops conducted by Roshan Taneja, his mother's drama coach, and Anupam Kher. He picked up interesting skills such as horse riding (owing to his presence on the sets of *Mard*) and fighting. Being a part of ABCL when *Major Saab* was under production gave him the chance to learn filmmaking. 'I did everything. I made tea, delivered food, carried bags, drove artistes to work, woke them up in the morning. I loved it. It taught me a lot. Till then I had thought the spot boy was someone who worked with the spotlight,' he says.

While amassing these varied skills, the wait continued for the big break. Finally, feeling stuck and edgy, he called his friend Rakeysh Mehra, who had directed Amitabh Bachchan in the BPL advertisements. They co-wrote a screenplay on India-Pakistan unity called *Samjhauta Express*, which was to be made into a small budget film. Unfortunately that did not take off, though years later Rakeysh did produce a film with Abhishek and Sonam Kapoor (daughter of Anil Kapoor) in the lead—*Delhi-6*. Sonam enjoyed working with Abhishek so much that she confessed in an interview that appeared in *Filmfare*: 'I want to work with Abhishek in every film, but the question is, does he want to work in every film with me?' JP Dutta decided to launch him in *Aakhri Mogul*, which was shelved for *Refugee*.

The year was 2000 and JP Dutta's war drama was a highly anticipated film; it was also launching two star kids—Kareena Kapoor and Abhishek Bachchan. Owing to the buzz around it, the movie opened to an excellent response but it turned out to be just about average. This spelt struggle for Abhishek who had to return the advance money that several producers had paid him. Critics, however, appreciated Abhishek's performance. According to Taran Adarsh of *Bollywood Hungama*, '[Abhishek] has all it takes to emerge a competent actor in years to come. Even though this was his debut

Kareena Kapoor, who was Abhishek's first heroine in Refugee.

film, Abhishek came across as a fine actor who lived up to his family name.' Another revered film critic, Anupama Chopra, wrote:

> All the Dutta trademarks are here—sweeping locales, strong performances, scale and a poetic musical score. Debutants Abhishek Bachchan and Kareena Kapoor play lovers on opposite sides of the border. She is Naaz, a Bangladeshi refugee living in Pakistan and he, an orphan of indeterminate religion, only known as 'Refugee'. He helps other refugees cross the perilous Raan of Kutch. As he navigates Naaz's family to Pakistan, the two fall in love. Dutta works hard and the sweat shows in every frame. Bachchan, who bears the onerous weight of his father's legend, isn't the instant star that Hrithik Roshan is. He has a slow charm and a smouldering intensity but needs to be more consistent. He is inexplicably limp in some scenes and exceedingly good in others.

Apart from the critics, Abhishek was appreciated as an actor by both JP Dutta and Kareena. Dutta shared in an interview as to why he chose Abhishek and Kareena:

> We had been working on a film for Abhishek which was to be produced by ABCL earlier. When that didn't happen and I walked up to them to cast Abhishek, they already knew my body of work. The Bachchans, too, were not looking at the usual masala film to launch their son. That's why there was a mutual respect when we decided to work together. I needed faces which were without the shadow of any other image they had built up earlier. I did not have a reference point for this subject, so I needed totally new faces ... He absolutely lived up to my expectations! I always believed that he had the makings of a great actor. The boy is a natural. He has sincerity, he has maturity, and he has the presence. And no, he isn't too suave. He can look hungry when required. He can look lean. He doesn't have a style to talk of at the moment, he has no mannerisms, nothing. He's just like the boy next door, he's so natural. He's intense and can look very endearing—the way he speaks, the way he smiles—you feel like holding him in your arms and saying, 'God bless you!'

The first scene Abhishek and Kareena shot was a romantic one: 'Abhishek and I were very comfortable from Day One because he is a close friend of mine. The chemistry was there right from the word go,' said Kareena, who went on to add, 'As a person he is wonderful ...' His father and mentor, also his strongest critic, commented:

> I watched *Refugee* a little earlier before its release. I liked the film and the concept of the story. Mr Dutta is a brilliant director. As far as Abhishek is concerned, I think he was okay but he has to learn a lot more. He is, however, improving with each and every picture. Experience counts in this trade. He has improved a lot in *Dhaai Akshar Prem Ke* [Abhishek's second film, released the same year as *Refugee*, with Aishwarya Rai as his co-star]. I liked the movie but unfortunately the audience thought otherwise.

'You live and learn. Yes, there was a sense of carelessness earlier,' confessed Abhishek in an interview that appeared in *India Today*. 'But when you go out there every Friday and get smacked on the face, you learn along the way.' On 30 June 2013, Abhishek tweeted that it has been 13 years since the release of *Refugee* and it has been a fun ride so far. He

Above: India Today *recognises Abhishek's talent and versatility.*

*Left: Abhishek referred to Kareena and himself as two very scared, nervous and hopeful debutants (*Refugee*).*

Getting ready for his first press conference.

thanked everyone for the immense love, faith, belief, support and tolerance: 'I would not be here without you!' He went on to add: 'Memories of the premiere of the film are still so vivid. The great Liberty cinema, almost the entire film industry, the media. And, amidst all this pageantry and excitement, two very scared, nervous and hopeful debutants, Kareena and myself. Great memories!'

'Not bad,' is how Abhishek describes his 14 years in Bollywood and 55-odd films. For him the journey, though fun, came with its share of failures, challenges and low moments. His career graph reflects a roller-coaster ride. There was an initial phase where he doled out 17 flops in a row. His films, from *Tera Jadoo Chal Gayaa* to *Haan Maine Bhi Pyaar Kiya Hai*, fared badly. Competition made the scenario tough—another star scion, Hrithik Roshan, also began his career at the same time with the super hit, *Kaho Naa ... Pyaar*

Co-star Aishwarya Rai went on to become his wife in real life.

Hai. The lowest points of Abhishek's career were the eight-month delay in distributing and the sordid failure of his friend Apoorva Lakhia's *Mumbai Se Aaya Mera Dost*. Abhishek attributes these failures to the high expectations and, characteristically honest, he admits, 'When I look back at *Refugee*, I think it was my worst performance.' The media hype was even more daunting. The critics, too, were relentless: 'They didn't like my hair, my make-up, my dress sense, my diction. They thought I was wooden, couldn't dance.' But he wasn't ever defensive because he believes that critics tell you what you should be doing. 'It got to a point where the Friday of my release was like another one biting the dust. You start doubting your capability and saying maybe this is the wrong profession for you,' he shares. His parents were his pillar; their faith in him was unflinching: 'They were just fantastic. My dad used to say, "Just keep working". It wouldn't give me time to think and sit at home to mope. Then he said, you are in front of the camera, improving every day. I just took on whatever work was given to me and did my best.'

With Rani Mukerji in Kabhi Alvida Naa Kehna.

According to Mani Ratnam, Abhishek keeps growing with every film by leaps and bounds.
Designed by Nilesh Vede

A still from Shararat, *2002.*

And then came *Yuva*: 'I know what my shortcomings were in my previous films, but I believe that filmmaking is a collective process. Everyone's perception about me changed after *Yuva*.' It was Mani Ratnam who put Abhishek in a completely different league. His performance as the angry hit man, Lallan, was the turning point of his career. Abhishek remembers the day Ratnam called him for *Yuva*:

It was 1 March 2003. Ajay [Devgn] and I were shooting an action sequence for *Zameen*. He dropped me at the hotel. Mani was calling me and I didn't pick up the phone. I don't take a call unless I recognise the number that flashes on my screen as people uselessly call and disturb me. Then Shaad [Ali], a dear friend of mine and his [former] assistant, called me. He told me Mani Sir wanted to get in touch with me. I asked why. He said Mani Sir wanted to meet me as he was in Mumbai. I said okay. When we met, Mani narrated the story of *Yuva*. He then asked me whether I would like to work with him. I thought that was a bit weird, funny and a bit sublime. I agreed immediately. That is how it happened.

His role as Lallan was praised by the critics and he was awarded the Filmfare Best Supporting Actor Award, IIFA Best Supporting Actor Award and Stardust Star of the Year Award—Male. It was this performance that gave the industry a glimpse of his potential. Even the media expressed that, with *Yuva*, he had come into his own and had delivered beyond expectations. 'Until I saw *Yuva*, even I'd lost hope in Abhishek,' noted Karan Johar. 'I thought, Is this the right career for him?' And this is what his co-star Rani Mukerji had to say: 'Abhishek Bachchan is such a sweetheart. He's rocking in *Yuva*. I think that he's got the best role.' Ratnam's association with Abhishek grew manifold post-*Yuva*, giving way to *Guru* and *Raavan*. In an interview with Bollywood.com, the director spoke at length about Abhishek and his skills as an actor:

> Every time I worked with him, he had drastically different characters and each time he delivered. He is tremendous to work with. Abhishek is growing with every film. He is growing by leaps and bounds. Although I can only talk about him since *Yuva*, it was when I first interacted with him. Even then I did not do something very drastic, we just made him play the character without worrying about anything. In *Raavan* his character is much larger than life—it needed a bigger portrayal, flamboyance. He has been able to do it convincingly.

With Antara Mali in Naach, *directed by Ram Gopal Varma.*

Abhishek perceives *Yuva* as a very special film that changed it all for him; with it came a whole new world of opportunities. Ram Gopal Varma approached him for *Naach*: 'I think Abhishek is a terrific actor. In fact, he took me by surprise. I saw some portions of *Main Prem Ki Diwani Hoon*—I just liked his demeanour, I liked the fact that he had some dignity ... I just came out during the interval, called him and said, "I want to make a film, I want to make a love story with you."' His performances in *Phir Milenge* and *Rakht* were intense but both movies did not do well at the box office.

Facing page: With Rani Mukerji in Bas Itna Sa Khwaab Hai.

Right and below: Abhishek's role in Raavan *(co-starring Aishwarya Rai) won him a lot of praise.*

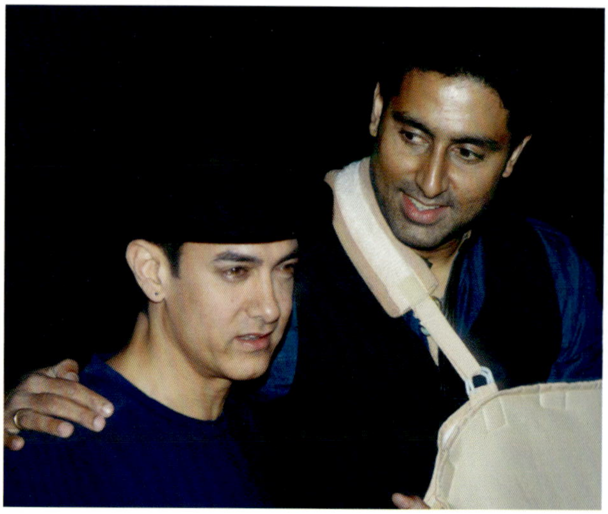

Abhishek (seen here with Aamir Khan) has played the part of a cool cop in all the Dhoom *movies.*

In 2004 came *Dhoom*, a fast-paced police-thief drama made under the Yash Raj banner and directed by Sanjay Gadhvi. Abhishek played the character of a cool cop in this multi-starrer venture, which turned out to be one of Bollywood's most successful series. ACP Jai Dixit and Ali (Abhishek and Uday Chopra, respectively) have featured in all the *Dhoom* movies. In an interview prior to the release of *Dhoom*, Abhishek said:

> I hope the audience has as much fun watching it as we had making it. When you put Uday Chopra, John Abraham, Esha Deol, Rimi Sen and me on the same sets, there is bound to be a lot of *dhoom*! It was a pleasure working with them. Uday is a very, very old friend of mine. We have virtually grown up together and helped each other whenever necessary. It was wonderful to finally face the camera with him. There isn't a dull moment when he's around. He loves to improvise. John Abraham has been a revelation. When you see his physicality, it is very easy to form an opinion about him. Far from being brawny and intimidating, he is gentle and soft-spoken. I have worked with Esha Deol before in *LOC Kargil*. She is opposite Uday, so we hardly met during the shooting. But Rimi, who plays my wife in the film, was a giggle expert! Each time she was around she would make us laugh with her giggles. The whole team was very young and enthusiastic. We gelled perfectly. I hope that chemistry shows.

And, two years later, came *Dhoom 2*. The movie also starred Aishwarya Rai who played a sexy, suave thief and the love interest of Hrithik Roshan. Bipasha

Basu added to the smouldering heat the movie exuded. It was internationally appreciated for its stunts. Rachel Saltz of *The New York Times* wrote, 'The pleasure principle is palpable in the giddy, slick *Dhoom 2*, a satisfying example of the new, thoroughly modern Bollywood. The film is shot in sharp, primary colours, with sophisticated stunts, exotic location hopping and songs sung partly in English.' Hrithik, who played the part of Aryan, said in an interview with IBN Live in 2006, 'I'm not saying this for effect, but Abhishek really inspires me. He has the potential to be one of our truly great actors. In fact, we've made a pact—Abhishek and I will do one film together every two years.'

'I had worked with Hrithik earlier during a world tour. Hrithik himself says he has loosened up a lot since then. He had lots of fun in *Dhoom*,' observed Aishwarya. 'As for Abhishek, I've known him much, much longer. He's always having fun on the sets. It relaxes him and makes the atmosphere on the sets far more convivial.' In 2013, the series doled out its blockbuster *Dhoom 3*, which touched the surreal number of Rs 300 crore. It featured Aamir Khan and Katrina Kaif along with Abhishek and Uday. 'I don't think the intention was to break any records but to make *Dhoom 3* as entertaining as possible,' says Abhishek. 'Of course, I am extremely happy that we managed to live up to our promise to our audiences and make an extraordinary film. The year did end with a *dhoom*. I'm glad that so many people enjoyed the film.' But, of the three, he has a favourite—*Dhoom 2*: 'Because it has everything—great music, good plot, characterisation, cinematography, locations and so on! All three

Dhoom 3 *proved to be a real blockbuster.*

*Abhishek can handle the comic (*Bunty Aur Babli*) and the dramatic (*Raavan*) with equal ease.*

Right: Seen with Mani Ratnam during the shooting of Raavan.

Dhooms are very different from each other and though it's not fair to compare them, I enjoyed doing *Dhoom 2* the most!'

Abhishek received a lot of criticism for his appearance in *Dhoom 2* and hence he worked extra hard on his physique for the sequel. The explanation for this lack of fitness was the fact that he had to put on 20 kg for his role in *Guru*. He readily agrees that Jai Dixit is very much a part of him: 'I can do Jai Dixit in my sleep, most of the prep for the film was in getting the physicality right. *Dhoom*, for me, is an emotional experience, as it was my first success ...'

The turnaround had happened and more success was bound to follow. His versatility as an actor was evident when he began experimenting and taking up character-specific roles. Leaving his brooding image behind, he portrayed the wannabe tycoon Rakesh aka Bunty from Fursatganj in *Bunty Aur Babli*. Abhishek calls it escapist cinema at its best: 'The average man and woman identify with Rani and me. We're stifled by the environment that we're born and brought up in. Our efforts to break away from the small-town environment will be understood by every member of the audience.' The song 'Kajra re' was an instant hit.

His comic talent got further honed in movies such as *Bluffmaster!*, *Dostana*, *Bol Bachchan* and *Happy New Year*. And though his co-stars—Rani, Riteish Deshmukh, Priyanka Chopra and several others—have spoken about the special chemistry they share with Abhishek and the ease of working with him,

it was John Abraham who remarked, accompanied by a wink, 'My chemistry with Abhishek [in *Dostana*] will be admired as the best until now between co-stars.' Abhishek reciprocated the feeling: 'Among all co-stars, I think John and I share the best, the most amazing chemistry.' Abhishek was awarded the IIFA Best Comedian Award for *Dostana*.

He entered the Rs 100 crore club with *Bol Bachchan*. In an interview that appeared in *Filmfare*, September 2012 issue, Abhishek said that this means that he needs to work even harder: 'I don't take the membership of this club lightly. The 100 crore club is like the silver jubilees and golden jubilees that the films celebrated earlier. Every actor is not lucky to win the love of the audience. When you get that love you need to respect and safeguard it.' In the movie Abhishek's character brought back memories of *Golmaal* as he played a double role to fool Ajay Devgn. One of the characters he plays with great ease is that of a Kathak dancer, a role that has got him a huge amount of appreciation. How did he manage this feat? To this, Abhishek replies:

> We didn't want to portray a caricature and poke fun at anyone. Comedy needs a serious approach. It should stem from the situation. If the Kathak dancer, Abbas, had not presented himself seriously, it wouldn't have been funny. Neither is he a Kathak dancer nor can he dance. What the audience finds funny is that the guy is trapped in a situation and he's making an effort to work his way out. I based the other character, that of Abhishek Bachchan, on Raja, a boy who worked on the sets of *Bol Bachchan*. Raja's walk, talk was imbibed in the character. You'll find

Abhishek with co-stars John Abraham and Priyanka Chopra in Dostana.

Shooting in Jaipur for Rohit Shetty's Bol Bachchan.

> that Abhishek's character is far more serious than Abbas'. Since it is Rohit's [Rohit Shetty] film, people tend to believe we don't take it seriously. But a lot of hard work goes in a comedy.

Even senior actors in the industry such as Waheeda Rehman, who played the part of his grandmother in *Delhi-6*, have praised his performance. 'Abhishek, among other things, definitely displayed a flair for the comic and pulled off movies like *Bol Bachchan* with great élan,' said Waheeda.

Sharing screen space with him were Ajay Devgn, Asin Thottumkal and Prachi Desai. 'Since Abhishek and I have known each other for years, the chemistry on screen is outstanding,' said Ajay. 'So many people have told me that we look good together on screen. Real-life bonding helps.' Asin, who played the role of his sister, admitted that of all the co-stars she has worked with, Abhishek is the perkiest and liveliest on the sets: 'With him around, there is a lot of fun and it wasn't any different for me. We haven't been paired opposite each other in the film but it would be great when that happens some day.'

Abhishek's style and understanding of comedy versus the comedy that *Bol Bachchan* required were two completely different genres:

> My style of comedy is more deadpan and straight-faced whereas the comedy that I did in the film was very demanding, as a lot of energy was required. We had to keep our energy levels high all the time. It took me a week to adapt to *Bol Bachchan*. The first week of shooting was really tough for me. I came with a particular mindset for the film and Rohit wanted something exactly opposite to it. I thought this will be the easiest film to do and it turned out to be the most difficult film of my career. It looks like a fun film and I thought it is a comedy film which I will enjoy, but I was proved completely wrong. I told Ajay if the film does well he has to send me on a holiday. Ajay and Rohit taught me that there is a pitch behind every film and you have to match it. I cannot repeat my characters as it will not suit the script. My style of comedy was very different from what *Bol Bachchan* required me to do. The two literally made me unlearn what I already knew and adopt a different style of comedy, which was very difficult for me.

In an interview to *Filmfare*, Abhishek compared films to a *thali* (plate), in which everything is included—action, drama, romance, tragedy, comedy, songs. 'I am at ease in all genres,' he said. While Abbas and Bunty flaunt the funny side of Abhishek, we have *Sarkar* and *Sarkar Raj*, which portray him in a completely different light and bring forth a brooding and strong character, Shankar Nagre.

After having cast Abhishek in *Naach*, Ram Gopal Varma approached the father-son duo for a politically intense family drama, loosely based on the life of Bal Thackeray. According to Ram Gopal Varma:

> Abhishek has never been put in a role he is made for, which his forte is. And he fits into *Sarkar*. Frankly, after finishing the film and seeing it—even though this is a first-time genre for Abhishek—I myself can't make up my mind about who is better. Like a guy who saw the film mentioned, 'Picture *dekh ke pata nahin lagta ki kaun kiska baap hai* [You can't make out who is whose father]!' I just loved that line, and I feel the same way. My point is that Amitabh Bachchan you've seen. You've seen him over the years in so many roles, so many films, that you will have a traditional expectation. Abhishek we haven't seen that much. He gives a certain twist to how Amitabh Bachchan would have played it in his younger days. Now,

Amitabh and Abhishek both excelled themselves in Sarkar.

this is something I haven't seen, so for me the excitement of seeing Abhishek doing that is greater than the excitement of seeing Amitabh doing that. I always felt that Abhishek came at a time when he was miscast. The trend was towards those NRI [Non-Resident Indian] romances, and his personality, his demeanour, doesn't fit into those. So in a movie like *Sarkar*, he is in the kind of role that I, or even you, would actually like to see Abhishek.

To this Abhishek retaliated:

Ramu saying I'm better than Dad has got to be the biggest joke of the century. You have to see Dad in *Sarkar* to know how outstanding he is. I am his biggest fan, he's getting better with every performance. When I saw the first cut of *Sarkar*, I dropped everything and called him suggesting we meet immediately. I was no longer his son. I was this huge fan who needed to connect with the greatest actor of the land.

The Senior Bachchan on his son's performance in *Sarkar*:

> It's a delight to me because I'm working with Abhishek—technically this was the first film we did together, at least we took our first shot together in this film. It's very exciting to see Abhishek succeed. It's something that every father hopes for. It's wonderful to see your own progeny, your own children doing well. Especially Abhishek, who has been through a great amount of turmoil and strife, and I'm happy that it is behind him, and he's been able to come up entirely on his own effort. He's managed to stand on his own feet. And that feels good. I think, as an actor and a co-star, Abhishek is very promising. I think he still has a long way to go, but it's encouraging to see that with each film he makes an improvement, takes big steps forward. I think he has great presence, and I think he needs more directors like Ram Gopal Varma.

A still from Sarkar Raj.

Sarkar Raj followed, which also featured Aishwarya Rai. It was a power-packed casting and the movie saw more hues of Abhishek, playing Shankar Nagre. His ability to get into the skin of the character was appreciated by all. Equally encouraging was the fact that the film did great business in India and overseas.

Among the movies that Abhishek has done with his father are *Jhoom Barabar Jhoom* and *Kabhi Alvida Naa Kehna (KANK)*. 'I love working with Abhishek, he is a total nut ... he is full of life and brings a mad energy and zest to the movie [*Jhoom Barabar Jhoom*],' said co-star Preity Zinta.

'I think that the relationship Dad and I had in *KANK* was similar to what we're like in real life, because we truly are best friends. You know, we do everything together,' observes Abhishek. 'Since I was a child, he's treated me like a friend.' He confessed in an interview that appeared in *DNA* that one of his life's toughest scenes was from *KANK*:

> In a particular scene I meet Rani [Mukerji] for the first time after we have split up and I have to inform her that my dad is dead and hand over his photograph. My dad [Amitabh] is playing that character and it's his photograph that I am holding

Facing page: Having fun doing a balancing act during a shooting.

Left: With Aishwarya Rai in Rohan Sippy's Kuch Naa Kaho.

in my hand. It was the most difficult scene of my life. There are few moments in every actor's life where it's more personal than acting. The scene started and I was holding my dad's picture and saying that he is dead. After the scene I just broke down and started crying. I was sitting in a corner and Karan [Johar] came up to me as he understood what I was feeling. He just hugged me as he, too, was missing his dad. He got teary-eyed; even Rani started crying looking at us. It was too special. Mickey [Contractor] took me for a long drive after that where I told him I am in love with Aishwarya. We were not dating back then.

The journey of the actor was picking up pace and then came a movie that defined the peak of his career; a movie whose brilliance can be heavily attributed to Abhishek's performance and Mani Ratnam's genius: *Guru* (2007). Loosely based on the life of Dhirubhai Ambani, this was a film that unabashedly belonged to Abhishek. Remembers Ratnam:

> When I started writing the screenplay, he was the first person I thought of. Then I told him this is what I am planning and if he is interested, I want three to four months at a stretch because I need him to be the character. I think he looked right for me. The fact that he has done *Yuva* just meant we worked well together. We know that we can deliver together. That makes a working relationship easier. It was an instinct that told me he was the right person and I followed the instinct.

For Abhishek, Ratnam is special: 'When he is directing a film, an actor doesn't need to ask for anything else ... He is truly a genius and deserves every bit of the credit that he gets.' Abhishek had to put on a lot of weight to play the character of Gurukant Desai, which surely was a risk since he was by then a hot favourite with the female audience but, for him, it is the role and not the star value that is important:

> *Guru* is a film that has been very demanding, very complex, but a film that has been very rewarding eventually. I don't think actors work for vanity; I think we work to enact an interesting character. We do what the character demands from us. We don't go with a certain kind of thinking, at least I never think that, 'My God, I shouldn't put on weight' or 'I shouldn't look old' or any such other conceptions because I think that the audience won't like it. The audience comes in to watch a film, to see the performance and to get entertained. So you have to do whatever needs to be done in order to achieve that. In a film like *Guru*, the physical aspect of the way he looked is very important to the narrative of the story. Hence you do what it takes. You have to prepare for every film ... I had to undergo certain changes like ageing and putting on weight.

Striking a stylish pose.
Photo courtesy: Flying Machine

But, for Abhishek, the best praise came when his father admitted that, in his place, he would not have been able to play the role as effectively, adding that he was proud of him. Amitabh wrote in his biography: 'When a father loses to his son, it is his greatest victory. I've lost to my son and I'm the happiest father alive. Abhishek is phenomenal ... I have been choked with emotion ever since

Even senior actors in the industry such as Waheeda Rehman, who played the part of his grandmother in Delhi-6, *have praised his performance.*

I emerged from the theatre and still am. This is a role of a lifetime for him and he has given a performance of a lifetime. It's a role any actor worth his salt would die for and it's a performance that any actor worth his salt will envy.'

Dus, *Delhi-6* and *Paa* followed. R Balki's *Paa* came with a twist of role reversal, with Abhishek playing reel-life father to his real-life father, Amitabh. And though the latter's performance as a progeria patient was exceptional, Abhishek's restrained role as a young politician and inadvertent dad received a fair share of praise as well. He is, however, all praise for Amitabh:

> To see my dad play the role of a person suffering from the condition was an unusual experience. On the first day, when we had the look test and Dad came out in his make-up, I didn't recognise him. It took me 10 minutes to realise that he was the man standing right next to me, and I had been looking for him all around. That was weird! But playing dad to him wasn't that weird. It was quite easy actually. Maybe because the dad-son relationship is more of friendship in the film. Besides, at the end of the day, we are just actors doing a job.
>
> Though Auro, the 12-year-old character in the film, is shown to be suffering from the condition, the film isn't really about progeria. We haven't delved into the many hardships that these unfortunate children have to live through; rather we have tried to show a happy, active child, who has a zest for life. Auro is a fun character; without being frivolous. We have made a conscious effort not to use progeria as a marketing point. We are aware of the 'progeria family' based in Kolkata; we have seen the documentary on them, too ... But ours is only a film, which takes necessary cinematic liberties in the portrayal of the character.

Another commendable success, *Happy New Year* (2014), directed by Farah Khan, showcased his versatility. 'Nandu is the most outrageous character I have ever played. I like to take on work that pushes me as an actor,' says Abhishek. 'We had to create the character from scratch. Farah and I spent a good one year on it before filming. People who generally don't perceive comic roles as hard work, don't know anything about filmmaking.' He won the Entertainer of the Year Award and Best Supporting Actor Award at Masala Awards 2014 in Dubai for his portrayal of the drunk, unfocused loser whose comic timing is impeccable.

Facing page: With Vidya Balan in R Balki's Paa*, where Abhishek played the role of Amitabh's father.*

Abhishek has unflinchingly worked in multi-starrer movies without any worry of sharing screen space: 'I don't have that kind of ego. And it's not just because I have worked with senior actors such as Aamir Khan, Shah Rukh Khan and Ajay Devgn,' he is quick to point out. 'If you look at my career, I have acted in many ensemble cast films with my contemporaries such as Hrithik Roshan and John Abraham.'

The future holds a lot of promise, with some interesting projects in hand, including *Housefull 3, Dostana 2, Time Machine* and *Biscuit*. Abhishek is passionate about making a biopic based on the life of his grandfather Harivanshrai Bachchan: 'I like biopics and am currently working on two of them. I enjoy the creative and acting process which goes into biopics. The character I would really love to play would be my grandfather.'

With Shah Rukh Khan and Deepika Padukone during a television interview to promote Happy New Year.

The Happy New Year *team.*

Abhishek has taken it all in his stride—struggles and successes, highs and lows—viewing them as necessary for growth. Without them, he says, the journey would be terribly boring: 'You have to have a bit of everything, that's what makes life so exciting!'

HITS & MISSES

NARENDRA KUSNUR

It was the year 2000, and huge expectations were pinned on the new stars Abhishek Bachchan and Kareena Kapoor. Both of them impressed the critics and the cinema audiences, but what stood out in JP Dutta's *Refugee* was its music. Composed by Anu Malik and written by Javed Akhtar, the songs 'Panchchi nadiya', 'Aisa lagta hai', 'Mere humsafar', 'Raat ki hatheli par' and 'Taal pe jab' were picturised on the lead pair. Barring 'Raat ki hatheli par', all the others were sung by Sonu Nigam.

Abhishek's career got off to a musical start and his early films had decent music.

Abhishek's career had got off to a musical start, and the film went on to win the National Award for best music direction; 'Panchchi nadiya' got the award for best lyrics. It seemed the actor would be flooded with romantic roles, and thus have a string of love songs filmed on him. But, looking back over the past 14 years, Abhishek has actually got a good mix of ballads, comedy songs and action-oriented songs. Some of the hits he has enacted include the *Kuch Naa Kaho* title track; 'Say na say na' and 'Right here right now' from *Bluffmaster*; 'Kabhi neem neem' from *Yuva*; 'Kajra re' (*Bunty Aur Babli*); 'Dilbar shikdum' (*Dhoom*); 'Dus bahane' and 'Deedaar de' (*Dus*); 'Masakali' (*Delhi-6*); 'Where's the party tonight?' (*Kabhi Alvida Naa Kehna*); 'Desi girl' (*Dostana*) and 'Nach le nach le' (*Bol Bachchan*).

The music in Refugee *was well appreciated and the film then went on to win the National Award for best music direction.*

If one looks chronologically at Abhishek's films, *Refugee* was followed by two films with decent music. In *Tera Jadoo Chal Gayaa*, music director Ismail Darbar had Sonu Nigam and Chitra render the title track. Sonu and Kavita Krishnamurthy sang the qawwali-influenced 'Qayamat ho qayamat ho' and Babul Supriyo did 'Chori chori chupke'. All three songs had Abhishek show his dance moves. Next came *Dhaai Akshar Prem Ke*, the first film featuring Abhishek and Aishwarya. The music was by Jatin-Lalit, who consistently used Babul Supriyo, barring one song by KK. It had hummable tunes in the title track, 'Do lafzon mein' and 'Yeh sama yeh nazaare'.

There have been several ups and downs after that. In 2001, Abhishek had only one release, *Bus Itna Sa Khwab Hai*, which flopped. The very next year,

Two hit songs (by Sonu Nigam) were picturised on Abhishek in Shararat *(left). His more recent* Delhi-6 *(Abhishek seen with Rishi Kapoor and director Rakeysh Omprakash Mehra) had a couple of wonderful songs as well.*

however, he enacted two wonderful songs, 'Kuch tum kaho' and 'Mehki hawayein', sung by Sonu Nigam, in *Shararat*. Music was by Sajid-Wajid. Sonu Nigam also sang for him in Apoorva Lakhia's *Mumbai Se Aaya Mera Dost*, which had music by Anu Malik. Despite good reviews and the success of the tune 'Shaher ka jadoo re', the film did average business, and its songs were soon forgotten. Abhishek's next film was Sooraj Barjatya's *Main Prem Ki Diwani Hoon*, but most of the songs were picturised on the main lead, Hrithik Roshan. The film bombed at the box office.

One of Abhishek's biggest musical successes during that phase was Rohan Sippy's *Kuch Naa Kaho*, which also starred Aishwarya. Music was by Shankar-Ehsaan-Loy and lyrics by Javed Akhtar, who had a huge hit in the title track, sung by Sadhana Sargam and Shaan. The film had the fun song, 'ABBG'. The actor's next film, *Zameen*, also had a fun song—'Tere sang ek simple si coffee'. Composed by Himesh Reshammiya and written by Sameer, it was sung by Hema Sardesai and KK. Himesh also gave music for Abhishek's next movie, *Run*.

It was AR Rahman who gave Abhishek one of his biggest hits in the 2004 film *Yuva*. Though the song 'Kabhi neem neem' featured more of Rani Mukerji, it had some sensitive acting by Abhishek. The piece was sung by Madhushree and Rahman. In the same year, Pritam had his first super-success with *Dhoom*. The songs included the title track (which had only fleeting glimpses of Abhishek) and the Middle-Eastern flavoured 'Dilbar shikdum', sung by Shaan and Shreya Ghoshal. Abhishek's next musical hit was *Bunty Aur Babli*, which had music by

Shankar-Ehsaan-Loy. The song 'Kajra re', picturised on Aishwarya, Amitabh Bachchan and him and sung by Alisha Chinai, Shankar Mahadevan and Javed Ali, became an instant rage. Other songs such as 'Chup chup ke', 'Nach baliye' and the title track were picturised on Abhishek and Rani Mukerji.

In 2005, Vishal-Shekhar gave Abhishek some of his biggest hits. First came *Dus*, which had the rabble-rousing 'Dus bahane' and 'Deedaar de'. In the days of dance bars, these songs were a craze. Then there was *Bluffmaster*, with music by Vishal-Shekhar, Trickbaby and Sameeruddin. The film had the hits 'Say na say na', 'Sabse bada rupaiyya', 'Boro boro' and 'Right here right now', with Abhishek singing the last one with Sunidhi Chauhan.

In Karan Johar's 2006 film, *Kabhi Alvida Naa Kehna*, Abhishek was part of the group song 'Rock 'n' roll soniye', but, for him, the highlight was 'Where's the party tonight?' The music was by Shankar-Ehsaan-Loy. The trio of music directors again hit gold with *Jhoom Barabar Jhoom*, with four songs picturised on Abhishek, though their music in *Game* was average. The 2006 film *Umrao Jaan*, directed by JP Dutta with music by Anu Malik, had Abhishek appear in songs such as 'Jhoote ilzaam' and 'Main na mil sakoon jo tum se', but they were largely picturised on Aishwarya and sung by Alka Yagnik.

Aishwarya Rai in JP Dutta's Umrao Jaan, *where she co-starred with Abhishek.*

Clockwise from top left: A still from Ashutosh Gowariker's Khelein Hum Jee Jaan Sey; *getting ready to face the camera for* Delhi-6; *outside Siddhivinayak Temple, Mumbai.*

In the period between 2007 and 2010, AR Rahman gave the tunes for *Guru*, *Delhi-6* and *Raavan*. *Guru*'s hit song 'Tere bina', was sung by Rahman, Murtuza Khan, Quadir Khan and Chinmayee. The song's main line is also used in 'Aye hairathe', sung by Hariharan, Alka Yagnik and Rahman. *Delhi-6* is best known for 'Masakali', sung by Mohit Chauhan, and 'Rehna tu', rendered by Blaaze, Benny Dayal and Tanvi Shah, with the lines in French by Vivien Chaiz and Claire. The folksy 'Genda phool', sung by Rekha Bhardwaj, Shraddha Pandit, Sujata Majumdar and VN Mahathi, has Abhishek enacting a fun part. Though the 2010 film *Raavan* did not fare well commercially, it had good songs such as 'Behne de', sung by Karthik and Mohammed Irfan, 'Beera' by Vijay Prakash, Mustafa and Keerti Sagathia, and 'Ranjha ranjha' by Rekha Bhardwaj, Javed Ali and Anuradha Sriram.

Notable among Abhishek's films after 2008 are *Dostana*, where the song 'Desi girl' was picturised on him, John Abraham and Priyanka Chopra, and *Paa*, where Ilayaraja composed the songs 'Mudhi mudhi ittefaq se' and 'Gumm summ gumm'. However, his performance in the 2012 movie *Bol Bachchan* is best remembered for its comic brilliance. While the audience went wild over his dance number featuring a medley of old songs, the Sukhwinder Singh-Shreya Ghoshal 'Nach le nach le' hit a melodic note.

Besides his roles as a hero or supporting actor, Abhishek has done guest appearances in many films and, in some cases, he has appeared in songs as

'Masakali', sung by Mohit Chauhan and picturised on Sonam Kapoor in Delhi-6, *was a huge hit.*

well. These include 'Kya maine socha' in the 2004 film *Rakht* and 'Nobody like you' in the 2008 release *Mission Istanbul*. And though he has had his share of hit songs over the years, his biggest musical film was his debut, *Refugee*. Even today, many people think of 'Panchchi nadiya' and 'Aisa lagta hai' when they think of songs filmed on Abhishek.

(Narendra Kusnur is a renowned Mumbai-based music critic)

One in every six people on Earth is an Indian, and I look forward to the day when we can compete with the heavyweights of the sporting world and do well in the medal tally.

DIFFERENT GOALS

While acting is in his genes, sport is an identity he embraces and this has led Abhishek to be an aggressive sports entrepreneur. He is in the process of setting up a separate company to handle his ventures in the business of sports. What is unique about his sports entrepreneurship is that he has chosen to support one of the most neglected and yet glorious sports of India—kabaddi. Football is yet another sport that has received his overwhelming support and, recently, he has managed to set foot into basketball at an international level.

When did his affinity towards sports start? He stated in an interview:

> When we were growing up, we were not so much into watching television. Every Sunday, a bunch of us used to play cricket, football and *pithu* outside the gates of Prateeksha. Whenever Dad was around, he used to join us and teach me. But there is one game that I taught him and it is basketball. That's because at the time basketball wasn't played in India. I picked it up in my boarding school. In fact, I was the captain of the basketball team in school. But my Dad introduced me to sports in a big way. He introduced me to Brazilian football and Muhammad Ali too. I remember he used to collect these VHS tapes that had the recordings of

Abhishek has always been very active in sports, Modern School, New Delhi.

A sports entrepreneur, Abhishek has chosen to support one of the most neglected and yet glorious sports of India—kabaddi.

all the great games, so I saw the likes of Pele, Zico and Socrates in action. It just started from there and grew. That's how I started All Stars Football Club, where a group of like-minded football-loving guys get together and play for charity. I attribute a lot to sports in the shaping up of my personality.

His favourite sport is basketball and just recently he has achieved a great feat when it comes to the game. Abhishek attended the NBA (National Basketball Association) All-Star 2015 and participated in the Sprint NBA All-Star Celebrity Game in February at Madison Square Garden, New York, as a goodwill ambassador to the league. A self-proclaimed Los Angeles Lakers fan, he met NBA players and legends throughout the weekend and went behind the scenes at the NBA All-Star Saturday Night and the 64th NBA All-Star Game. He is the first-ever Indian to take part in the NBA All-Star Celebrity Game. 'I'm excited and honoured to be attending my first-ever NBA All-Star as a goodwill ambassador to the league,' he said. 'I know my trip will show

Abhishek, while visiting a school in Mumbai, could not resist playing with the eager students.

ALL
STARS

fans in India the excitement, energy and athletic ability of the NBA game and its players. Basketball is my first love, and I look forward to supporting basketball's continued growth in India.'

Displaying the true spirit of a sports entrepreneur, he has formed the Jaipur Pink Panthers kabaddi team and the Chennaiyin FC football team. 'If given an opportunity, I want to be a sportsman, even today. I want to promote the sport that is indigenous to India. Kabaddi is a matter of national pride. Why can't cricket, hockey, football and kabaddi be given equal platforms and co-exist? I believe that can happen,' he observes. The game is rooted to some fond childhood memories: 'When I was a child, my father and I would play kabaddi in our garden with my cousins. I think most Indians have played the game.'

A proud moment for Abhishek's Jaipur Pink Panthers kabaddi team.

Aishwarya Rai celebrates with the winning team.

His first glimpse of kabaddi was seeing his father play it in the movie, *Ganga Ki Saugandh*. The sports enthusiast in Abhishek was keen on supporting it and thus 'The Kabaddi Revolution' happened. An initiative of Marshal Sports, it has eminent personalities such as businessman Anand Mahindra, advertising guru Piyush Pandey, eminent lawyer Rajiv Luthra and commentator, compere and quizmaster Charu Sharma as its driving force. The games of this league were held on a 'home and away' format and its official broadcast partner, Star Sports, ensured that the audience enjoyed the live coverage of all the games at prime time daily. The responsibility of managing and marketing this prestigious event was given to the World Sports group.

What made Abhishek join this revolution? His answer, shared with Tellybuzz, comes straight from the heart:

> Charu came to me with the idea of Pro Kabaddi, and I was taken aback, knowing as to how we take the sport for granted. It's such a cheap sport. In cricket, you need a lot of equipment, even for football, which is still cheap, you need a ball, but every

parent can teach kabaddi to their child as all they need is a ground to play. We're a cricket-loving nation, including me, but that's a British sport. Hockey, too, is a British sport. As far as I know, kabaddi is the only Indian sport still played. So, when Charu spoke to me, he appealed first to the patriot in me, because I am a bit of a sentimentalist and this is 'our' sport. Also, the sportsmen who play kabaddi don't get the kind of facilities that the more accomplished sportsmen of the country get. The idea is to give these sportsmen the kind of infrastructure and recognition they deserve.

Left: Besides his family, Abhishek's effort to promote kabaddi in India has been supported by Sachin Tendulkar, Tina Munim, Kabir Bedi, among others.

Right: Seen with Ronnie Screwvala and his wife Zarina Mehta.

He thus decided to own the Jaipur team for the Pro Kabaddi League; it was named Jaipur Pink Panthers. His reasons for endorsing the game are many:

Why not kabaddi? It's a heritage sport. It is believed that it comes down from the times of the Mahabharata. They say that Abhimanyu's Chakravyuh—where one person was against seven—was a form of kabaddi. It is the only indigenous sport and there's no spotlight on it. It's looked upon as a rural sport but you'll be amazed to know that in Mumbai itself there are 450 kabaddi clubs! Do you know that India has won all five kabaddi World Cups and has won the Asian Games six times?

Commentator, compere and quizmaster Charu Sharma (left) and businessman Anand Mahindra (right) are also part of Abhishek's endeavour to popularise kabaddi on television.

PKL's first edition started on 26 July 2013. It attracted quite a lot of high-profile investors such as the GMR Group, the Kotak Group, and Kishore Biyani's Future Group. After buying the Jaipur franchise of this league, Abhishek expressed his joy in an interview:

> Having been a sportsman and, being a sports enthusiast, it's very exciting to be able to be a part of this endeavour. The sport of kabaddi is already immensely popular, through the league I hope we can take this great sport to a whole new horizon … Television is a huge audience base. I'm fairly confident that the stadiums will be packed, because it is a popular sport among the masses.

It was largely pegged that Abhishek's celebrity status is the reason he is a part of the initiative, an angle that he has strongly denied:

> I agree that when you add a celebrity to something, you attract eyeballs but we're not here for that. I'm not an actor here, I'm a sports enthusiast. I've told Charu earlier as well, that if you think that I'm a film actor and I'm just going to go to Jaipur and wave my hand, then no, that's not going to happen. I'm the owner of the team, and will be actively involved. And if I can use the little star status that I have to help the sport, I'll be stupid not to do it.

Abhishek with the members of his Chennaiyin FC football team.

AIYIN
Hero
INDIAN SUPER LEAGUE
CHENNAIYIN F.C.
TYKA

With Kiran Rao and son Azad at a football match (left); Abhishek enjoying a game of table tennis (right).

Facing page: Greeting football enthusiasts.

It is this dedication that ensured PKL's success. While the Indian Premier League (IPL), which is an immensely popular Twenty20 cricket competition, attracted 453 million eyeballs in the first 15 days, the FIFA World Cup was viewed by 129 million football lovers, the released data by Star Sports declared that PKL registered 288 million viewership. Abhishek, along with the other supporters of the league, have successfully broken the myth that kabaddi is a rural sport. He has a clear game plan:

> For the first three seasons I want to take the game to the urban youth in our country and try and make it as cool as football, cricket and tennis for them so that they pick it up. It's time we have a sports revolution in India. Middle-class India still thinks of sports only as a game. Even though cricket was always big in our country, there is no denying that IPL has revolutionised it even more and made it a viable career option for so many cricketers. Not every sportsman can play for the country and we have to think of them too. I'm hoping, with PKL, we can take kabaddi to the people.

This commitment paid off and the first season winners were Jaipur Pink Panthers. Abhishek couldn't believe that his team had won and he shared this thrill by tweeting, 'Last night feels like a dream ... All the hard work of the

boys, coach and staff came through. Thank you all for the unbelievable support! Any sport is made by the fans and kabaddi has awesome fans! Thank you for supporting Jaipur Pink Panthers.' Abhishek's joy was evident in the way he cheered his team to glory.

Just like kabaddi, Abhishek's first brush with football was due to his father. Talking about his earliest interest in football, in an interview with *The Times of India*, he says, 'My father introduced me to Brazilian football at a very early age. If I can remember correctly, I have been a fan of Brazilian football since the 1982 World Cup. Also, having studied in a British boarding school since the age of nine, as you can imagine, life revolved around football.'

But football got his attention as a sports entrepreneur when the Sun Group backed out from owning the Chennai football team. He immediately grabbed this opportunity to own a football team and bought it along with Vita Dani of Asian Paints. Mahendra Singh Dhoni owns a minority stake in the team as well. Buying a football franchise was a decision prompted by passion for Abhishek believes it would be difficult to drive the ISL if there is no passion. He is actively involved with the league and has attended all official functions; he even travelled to Rome to convince former World Player of the Year, Ronaldinho, to join the team. He is determined not to treat football like a fly-by-night operation: 'I'm a team owner who likes to be involved with the game. I like to travel with my team. It boosts their morale.'

Amitabh strongly upholds that it is initiatives such as ISL that will strengthen the game and its popularity in India. 'I do believe that this shall gradually grow into a most interesting and captivating sport in the years to come,' he wrote on his blog. Like always, Amitabh ensured his presence to support his son and his team by attending the match between Chennaiyin FC and Kerala Blasters.

Abhishek with Ranbir Kapoor at the opening of a match for the selection of Young Champs, a Reliance Foundation initiative.

Yet another football initiative that Abhishek has supported is BPL Live. He helped launch the event with a football match between his team of celebrities, All Stars Football Club (ASFC) and the Barclays Premiere League Legends, which includes Robbie Fowler, Emile Heskey and Lee Trundle. He has started following the Barclays Premier League since 1993 and is a staunch fan of Chelsea. In an interview with premierleague.com, he expressed his excitement at having played this match, 'What a pleasure and what a dream for some of my boys to get the opportunity to play with these absolute legends. Just to get to play with some of these people is absolutely brilliant. It's something we're very excited about.' His team included Ranbir Kapoor, Aditya Roy Kapoor and Dino Morea. Said Ranbir: 'We got well beaten but deservedly so. But it was great fun just to share the same pitch with some of these guys we idolised when we were younger.' 'These are very exciting times for football in India, we are going through a football revolution in the country and that is exactly what we needed,' observed Abhishek. 'Initiatives like this will make a huge difference. It helps connect with the fans, which is what they want. To get some of the greats of the game here is absolutely fantastic.'

Abhishek was invited to Rome for an Interreligious Match; he received the invitation from the former Inter Milan player Javier Zanetti. The match was named and initiated by the Pope himself and was held at the Olympic Stadium in Rome. The intent of the match was to harbour world peace through sports.

Revisiting Jamnabai, his old school in Mumbai.

This is not the first time that Abhishek has shown his love for the game. Previously, despite a busy schedule, the actor decided to fly to Rio de Janeiro, Brazil, in order to attend the semi-finals and finals of FIFA along with his father. In fact, Abhishek believes he has turned his father into a football fan and said in an interview with Bollywood.com, 'I had been to the Chelsea matches several times. But it was the first time for Pa. And I was excited, both by the thought of attending my favourite team's match and by the fact that my dad was so excited. We had a ball.'

He believes India has all the talent needed to be competitive in football but lacks on the infrastructure front and support for the game in general. He dreams of seeing the Indian team in the World Cup finals; he even goes on to set a goal that, by 2020, India should be a competitive football nation. When asked whether he is motivated by passion or business, he confessed:

> I'd be lying if I said that it's a 100 per cent passion project. Nobody wants to lose money ever. But I firmly believe that in order to do something well, there has to be passion involved. There's a line in *Bluffmaster*, which I told Rohan [Sippy] to put, where my character tells Boman [Irani], that if you don't have this [points to his heart], then there is no point of this [points to the head].

Abhishek is quick to emphasise that he is, and will always be, an actor first. But sport is a passion and he is glad to be involved in it: 'Luckily, I have so far been able to handle both and hope to continue doing so.' If given a chance, he would love to enact the roles of hockey player Major Dhyan Chand and his dear friend, cricketer Yuvraj Singh: 'Both are such extraordinary men and have led such incredible lives. Yuvraj is such a champion, a great human being and his story is full of triumph. It's amazing the way he keeps fighting back.' He had also once discussed with Rohan Sippy the possibility of making a movie about a bunch of slum children who want to play basketball. 'Maybe it's time to revisit the idea,' he says, wistfully. 'In our industry, there is a belief that sports films don't do well, but then we made *Lagaan*.'

A REAL HERO

BY AYAZ MEMON

There are lovers of sport and then there are those with a sporting instinct. Those belonging to the first category follow sport with a passion, keeping track of all records, statistics, performances and so on. They may also be players. Those belonging to the second category, however, not only have a passion for sport but also a distinctive feel for it, which transcends the scorebook and active participation. For them, sport is almost a spiritual pursuit.

There are millions in the first category; the second are rare. According to me, Abhishek Bachchan belongs to the second category. I say this not because he now owns two teams in Indian sports leagues (kabaddi and football). That is easily done by those who have the financial wherewithal; there are many rich people who acquire a sports team as a toy. A sporting instinct, on the other hand, demands something greater. It seeks personal humility and reverence for the sport and its practitioners, which is born not necessarily out of hero worship, but an acute understanding of what it takes to reach levels of excellence in any sport.

I discovered that Abhishek has a penchant for sport in the few times I have interviewed him. He would readily break into discussing a performance or the prospects of a team or player in some impending contest. That it probably runs

Always a winner—Abhishek making a stylish entry at the Trident hotel, Mumbai.

deeper—I must admit that this is a surmise—comes from a few interactions, most notably during the Olympic Games in 2012. As brand ambassador for Omega, he was invited to the watch company's party in central London one evening during the Games. He was a much-in-demand celebrity (showing the spread and power of Indian cinema), but I found Abhishek was reluctant to get any attention for himself. 'These are the real heroes, I am a fake,' he said, pointing to ace sprinter Justin Gatlin.

It takes conviction and maturity to acknowledge that your place in the pecking order of life may be highly exaggerated. In my opinion, sports stars exceed those who perform for the camera for the simple fact that there is no retake for the sportsperson. They live or die by the moment, unlike a film actor, who can

Always an enthusiast—posing with fans (facing page) and celebrating with his team (right).

work and improve on his 'shot' any number of times. This is a humbling truism that dawns only on a few. The manner in which Abhishek conducted himself that day was truly impressive. He preferred remaining in the background, letting, as he said, the 'real hero' get the attention.

This ability, I believe, has helped Abhishek enormously. His lineage is as intimidating as it is formidable. His parents are widely regarded as among the best actors in the history of Indian cinema. His wife, also an actor, is a global celebrity. From whatever I have understood, he has not let this affect his equanimity or outlook. It would be impossible not to get bothered at some time or the other when comparisons are made. But Abhishek does not seem to have let this become burdensome. He has been able to sort it out in his head and has the ability to live in his own skin. This is a singular achievement for anybody from any walk of life. It comes only to those who can look life in the eye and treat the lows and the highs with the same calm and composure. Without a sporting instinct, this would be impossible.

(Ayaz Memom is a leading journalist and cricket commentator)

I was lucky to have all four grandparents while growing up. I'm really very happy Aaradhya will have that.

ALL IN THE FAMILY

Abhishek would love to make a biopic on his grandfather's eventful life, but realises it is going to be a Herculean task, despite the research material available. Born on 27 November 1907 to a lower-middle-class family settled in Allahabad, Harivanshrai Bachchan was the first Indian citizen to have obtained a PhD in English Literature from Cambridge; he was also a Hindi scholar. He gave soulful philosophies the beauty of words and immortalised them for the world. An acclaimed writer and poet, his literary masterpiece *Madhushala* (1935) is part of a brilliant trilogy whose later editions included *Madhubala* (1936) and *Madhukalash* (1937). His 'Rang barse' (Yash Chopra's *Silsila*) is a song that is hummed even today. Financial crises, repeated criticism and the untimely death of his first wife pushed him into a creative stupor. The genesis of Harivanshrai's writing was extreme pain and suffering, which is reflected in his creations. He married Teji Suri in 1941 and they had two sons, Amitabh and Ajitabh.

Harivanshrai Bachchan (seen with son Amitabh on facing page) was an acclaimed writer and poet.

Shrivastav was Harivanshrai's actual surname, not Bachchan, which was his pen name. The name Bachchan was derived from 'Bacha', which his mother used to call him. 'Bachchan' means 'childlike always'; over time, his pen name became his surname and the 'Bachchan' legacy began. In 1976, he was honoured with the Padma Bhushan for his contribution to Hindi literature. He wrote his last poem in 1984, based on the assassination of the then Prime Minister Indira Gandhi. Harivanshrai passed away in 2003, at the age of 96, owing to respiratory problems. A postal stamp was released in his honour in 2003, soon after his death. 'A body of clay, a mind full of play, a moment's life,' is how he described himself.

A style icon of her time, the dynamic Teji Bachchan (1914–2007) belonged to an aristocratic family from Lyallpur district, which is now in Pakistan. She was a professor of Psychology and was involved with India's freedom struggle. Post-Independence she assumed the role of a social activist and also

Jaya and Amitabh with Harivanshrai and Teji Bachchan (left); Abhishek with his parents and grandmother (right).

worked as the director of the Film Finance Corporation in 1973. Teji was a commendable singer and a theatre actor. She was a close friend of Indira Gandhi. 'She had a charismatic personality and her reputation for style and aesthetics was so famous that we are told prominent families of Allahabad were in great anticipation of my mother arriving into the city,' remembers Amitabh. 'And even though my father lived in an environment of very limited means, she was always able to find time and money to get her children the trendiest clothes and dress up in style. So that's where I must have inherited my fondness for good clothes.'Apart from her academic credentials, Teji was a commendable singer and a theatre actor. She acted in a series of Shakespeare plays, translated by her husband into Hindi and even played the role of Lady Macbeth. 'I credit my religious belief to my grandparents, especially my grandmother, because she has taught us about Hinduism and other religions,' says Abhishek, adding, 'She used to tell us about the adventures of Lord Hanuman, which all of us still remember.' She passed away at the age of 93, in 2007.

Taroon Kumar Bhaduri and Indira Bhaduri, parents of Jaya Bachchan, are interesting personalities who have had a great influence on Abhishek's life as well. Taroon Kumar was a writer, journalist and stage artist in Jabalpur, where Jaya was born. On a recent trip to Bhopal, Amitabh had a special treat lined up for his granddaughter Aaradhya. He hired a chartered flight to take her to Jaya's hometown, so that she could meet her grandmother's family in the city of lakes. As he, Abhishek and Aishwarya, along with Aaradhya, reached Bhopal they went straight to Ansal Apartments, where Jaya's mother stays.

Abhishek claims to be a mama's boy: 'She is my mother. The word Ma is all-encompassing.' Jaya is a disciplinarian and said to be the one who has kept the family together:

> I'm an extremely strict mother. And it isn't because my children were susceptible to being spoilt. We never allowed that. My children and my brother-in-law's children grew up together. They played and ate together, went to the same school. They had a normal life. They knew their parents were celebrities—we didn't hide it from them. But they didn't know what that celebrity entailed. They were aware that there was public interest in them when they went out. But we made sure they grew up with the celebrity status being a normal state of being. We never had to explain their identity to them. Amitji and I have been honoured but never dazzled by our celebrity. As a couple, we've ensured that our children don't compromise or denigrate it.

'She taught me that you don't always have to be doing something in front of the camera to get attention,' notes Abhishek. 'You can hold the audience with a close-up shot, without twitching. You don't need to act.' Instilling the right values in her children was of paramount importance for Jaya: 'I keep telling

Abhishek readily admits that he has always been a mama's boy.

Facing page: Abhishek and Aishwarya in Dhaai Akshar Prem Ke.

Right: Amitabh and Jaya enact a romantic scene.

Jaya took a sabbatical to be with her children Abhishek and Shweta during their growing up years (left); a family portrait with Shweta's husband, Nikhil Nanda, on the extreme right, standing.

my son every single day, it doesn't matter if a film does well or not. What matters is a light boy saying 30 years later, "It was such a pleasure working with you".'

Born in 1948 to a Hindu-Bengali family, Jaya did her schooling at St. Joseph's Convent School, Bhopal, where she was the head girl and, in 1966, she was awarded for being the Best NCC Cadet in India. A gold medallist from the Film and Television Institute of India (FTII), Pune, Jaya made her debut in Satyajit Ray's *Mahanagar,* where she acted with Anil Chatterjee and Madhabi Mukherjee. Her big break in Bollywood was Hrishikesh Mukherjee's *Guddi.* Amitabh revealed on the popular television show, 'Rendezvous with Simi Garewal', that the first good look he had of Jaya was on the cover of a magazine. He had always wanted a woman who was a perfect blend of tradition and modernity, and he thought Jaya came across exactly like that in the picture. He also said that what really caught his attention was her beautiful eyes. It was much later that Hrishikesh Mukherjee came up with the script of *Guddi* and Amitabh was very excited at the prospect of being cast opposite her, but, after shooting for a few days, Amitabh was replaced by another actor. *Guddi* was a huge success and it brought Jaya to Mumbai. For long she was cast in the 'girl-next-door' image, then she began experimenting by taking up films such as *Bansi Birju*, *Ek Nazar*, *Jawani Deewani*, *Anamika*, *Koshish* and *Zanjeer*.

Amitabh and Jaya got married on 3 June 1973 and it was during the making of *Sholay* that their first child, Shweta, was born. In 1981, Jaya quit acting, revealing to Simi that, at that point in time, the prospect of having a family and spending time with the children came across as a much more interesting option for her. She also shared that she did not even once speak to Amitabh about this while taking the decision, highlighting, 'My children are the most important elements of my life, even more important than my husband.'

After her children grew up and were settled in their lives, Jaya returned to Bollywood. In 1998, she did Govind Nihalani's *Hazaar Chaurasi Ki Maa*, a film based on the Naxalite movement; she played Hrithik Roshan's mother in *Fiza*, for which she won the Filmfare Best Supporting Actress Award followed by *Kabhi Khushi Kabhie Gham*. She also received the Filmfare Best Supporting Actress Award for her performance in *Kal Ho Na Ho*. She entered politics and was elected as a Member of Parliament for representing the Samajwadi Party at the Rajya Sabha. She was re-elected in 2012 and continues to play an active part in Indian politics.

The three Bachchans appeared on Simi Garewal's television show, 'Rendezvous with Simi Garewal'.

Though a self-confessed disciplinarian, Jaya shares a very close bond with her children.

During the celebration of Amitabh's sixtieth birthday, who is seen here with Jaya, Abhishek and grandson Agastya.

Abhishek has always shared a very special bond with his father as well, whom he admires immensely: 'He is a complete rock star; he is younger than I am at heart. The amount of energy he has is amazing. He works 19 hours a day, I work 15 to 16 hours.' Amitabh said in an interview:

> I had decided even before he was born that if I had a son, he would be my friend ... I just like the idea of not treating him like a son so that I can talk freely with him on any issue, crack jokes, just be one with his thinking and he to be one with mine. He is very obedient. The moment you start sharing personal points of view with another individual, there is a closeness that comes and I share everything with him and so does he. And we talk about issues and we come to conclusions. When we get stuck, we go to his sister and then finally it comes to Jaya.

Abhishek emphasises, 'There can never be another Amitabh Bachchan. His preparation and dedication took him where he is. We can only emulate him and give our 100 per cent to our work.' It is widely believed that Abhishek has inherited style and sophistication from his father. He always knew his father

Says Abhishek of his father: 'He is a complete rock star; he is younger than I am at heart. The amount of energy he has is amazing.'

was a public figure but never did he feel that he was inaccessible to him. He never felt overshadowed by the phenomenon that is Amitabh Bachchan.

Born in Allahabad, Amitabh (means Everlasting light) was given his name by poet and novelist Sumitra Nandan Pant, who was staying with his parents at that time. After completing his education from Sherwood College, Nainital and Kirori Mal College, Delhi University, he moved to Kolkata to work for a shipping firm, Shaw and Wallace. Fortunately, his mother encouraged him to pursue his passion for acting and he left for Mumbai. A period of struggle followed as back then a dark, brooding, lanky persona was not considered to be hero material. In spite of having a rich baritone voice, Amitabh failed in an audition at the All India Radio! Ultimately, it was KA Abbas who gave him his first break in *Saat Hindustani* (1969); the film did not do well but his performance did not go unnoticed. In 1973, came *Zanjeer* and, suddenly, a star was discovered; it was the birth of 'The Angry Young Man'.

Amitabh worked with a host of directors in the 1970s and 80s, including BR Ishara, Shankar Mukherjee, Prakash Mehra, Yash Chopra, Hrishikesh Mukherjee and Manmohan Desai. He excelled in all kinds of roles—romantic,

In discussion with his chacha *Ajitabh (Amitabh's younger brother).*

Gauri and Shah Rukh Khan at a Diwali party hosted by the Bachchans.

comic, action. When he was gravely injured during the filming of *Coolie* in 1982, the entire nation prayed for his recovery. He has gone through several upheavals but has characteristically managed to emerge stronger after each setback. He has won many prestigious awards, including the Padma Vibhushan, which President Pranab Mukherjee presented him in 2015. In 1999, he was named BBC Superstar of the Millennium.

At the recent Big Star Entertainment Award ceremony, both father and son were nominated in different categories for their movies *Bhootnath* and *Happy New Year*, respectively. The two celebrated each other's success together on stage. Amitabh tweeted, 'There are very few occasions in life when father and son get decorated on the same platform, same time, same day! A moment of pride.'

Amitabh is a vegetarian who does not smoke or have tea or coffee, Coke or Pepsi, chocolates, alcohol, paan, rice, sweets. Abhishek shares a similar taste palate, 'We both would be content with our simple meal of dal, vegetables and all, but Mom is an adventurous foodie.'

Shweta has always been close to her younger brother and the two nurture memories of their magical childhood.

Abhishek's eternal partner-in-crime is his sister, Shweta: 'She has been like what any other elder sister will be to her brother. She is also a mother figure and friend.' The two have shared a magical childhood, teenage curiosities, youthful fun and mature conversations. In a recent interview given to a leading daily, Shweta talks about her brother:

> Ever since he was a boy, he wanted to act. He enjoyed going to the sets and struck up friendships with the entire unit, they indulged him and I remember him making a boy's game out of serious props like swords and hand pistols. The sets were truly his playground. At home he enacted action sequences with all his vigour, me and my hapless dolls and teddy bears bearing the brunt of his melodramatic fury. I correct myself, he didn't want to grow up to be an actor—he wanted to grow up and be Amitabh Bachchan! Today when I see him on screen, larger than life, it feels surreal, glimmers of his make-believe world of dangerous villains and man-eating monsters flash through my mind.

'Shweta and Abhishek have always surprised me with how well adjusted they are,' observes Amitabh. 'They studied abroad during their formative years. They could have gone wrong, being away from home. But they didn't and stayed rooted in the values inculcated by the family.' Shweta is an important support system of the family. She was never inclined towards acting as a career but, as her father said in an interview to *Filmfare*, 'Shweta is the best actor in the family. I think she missed out on her vocation in life. She is more academically inclined too and more worldly-wise than any other member of the house.'

With Shweta's husband Nikhil Nanda and children, Navya Naveli and Agastya.

She was a citizen journalist with CNN IBN and, in 2007, hosted 'NextGen', a series of interview shows aired on NDTV Profit. Shweta's passion for writing and journalism continue and she writes a regular column for *DNA After Hrs.* She is married to industrialist Nikhil Nanda, the son of Ritu Nanda (daughter of Raj Kapoor) and Rajan Nanda and lives in Delhi with her husband and two children, Navya Naveli and Agastya Nanda.

Abhishek refers to wife Aishwarya as his best friend. He recollects the first time they met: 'It was in August 1997. I was on a recce for my father's film *Mrityudaata* in Switzerland and she was shooting her first film, *Aur Pyaar Ho Gaya*. Bobby [Deol, her co-star] invited me to his hotel for dinner and Aishwarya was there.'

Abhishek considers his co-star and now wife, Aishwarya Rai, to be his best friend.

Tagged as the 'world's most beautiful woman', Aishwarya Rai Bachchan was born into a traditional South Indian family. She was a student of architecture before she took up modelling as a part-time job and was best known for her Pepsi commercial with Aamir Khan and Mahima Chaudhry. After being crowned Miss World 1994, she was flooded with film offers and went on to win the Filmfare Best Actress Award for her role in *Hum Dil De Chuke Sanam* in 1999. Aishwarya has an impressive line-up of films to her credit and is the first Indian actress to be on the jury of the Cannes Film Festival. Once, when asked about her ideal man in an interview, Aishwarya commented:

> My ideal man should be madly in love with me because I won't have it any other way. I am a total romantic at heart, so naturally, my ideal mate better be well versed in the art of romance. Not flirting, but romance. And there is quite a difference. I dig dignity. It is rare and priceless in a world that's so taken over by images and put-ons.

Her search ended when she found Abhishek, who, she says, is her source of inspiration: 'He is always so supportive. Whenever I am confused and don't know what to do, I look at him and he solves the duality in me like magic.'

How did this magic begin? Even though the two did a string of films together, each had their personal love lives. It is said that it was during the shooting of 'Kajra re' for

The world's most beautiful woman, Aishwarya Rai, 1994.

Aishwarya is like an anchor for me, says Abhishek of his wife.

Bunty Aur Babli that the chemistry between the two was noticed. They came closer while shooting for *Guru* and got married on 20 April 2007. During an interview with Oprah Winfrey, Abhishek shared, 'I was filming in New York for a movie and I used to stand on the balcony of my hotel room and wish that one day, wouldn't it be nice if I was together with her, married.' Several years later, when they were in New York after attending the premiere of *Guru* in Toronto, Abhishek took her to that balcony and proposed marriage. The ring he carried was a prop from the sets of *Guru*—the same ring that Abhishek had slipped on Aishwarya's finger in the film. He, in fact, had asked the producer if he could keep the ring for sentimental reasons.

Abhishek confessed in an interview with *DNA After Hrs*:

> Aishwarya is like an anchor for me. My parents had always given me freedom to do whatever I wanted. I was carefree. After marriage and my daughter's arrival I have become more responsible. Aishwarya is my buddy, a friend. I can discuss anything with her. Our relationship is not based on her being *the* Aishwarya Rai or me coming from an illustrious family. It is just about two people falling in love which was organically grown. We shot three back-to-back films for a year at that time. It started during *Guru*. We were meant to be, it is destiny.

A father since 16 November 2011, Abhishek has embraced this new role in his life wholeheartedly. Aaradhya Bachchan means everything to him, he enjoys every aspect of her growing up, from the first bubble bath to her first word. He feels that, at times, Aaradhya behaves older than him: 'She is a very easy, very happy and very loving kid. I will never do anything that will bring shame to my daughter today or 10 years down the line,' he declared in an interview (*DNA After Hrs*). As for his experience as a father, he told *People* magazine, 'Every parent has a special bond with his or her children. The greatest thing about parenting is [that] it's an instinct. On the arrival of your baby, it just kicks in. I'm just very happy spending time with her.'

Abhishek married his co-star Aishwarya on 20 April 2007.

The Bachchan power couples.

The name, Aaradhya, is derived from a Sanskrit word, which means one who is worshipped. Her name was announced by the Bachchan family officially, a special card was designed for the purpose. She is considered India's most famous baby, the dream of the paparazzi. Aaradhya celebrated her first birthday with her grandparents and parents at home; she received a BMW Mini Cooper as a gift from her doting dad. Her friends include Aamir Khan's son, Azad; Shilpa Shetty Kundra's son Viaan; Lara Dutta's daughter, Saira and Hrithik Roshan's sons, Hrehaan and Hridhaan.

Amitabh wrote on his blog:

> Aaradhya turns on the iPad to her favourite nursery rhymes programme all by herself ... picks up a remote whenever she can see one and points it to the TV in a pretense to put it on. What a fantastic generation of our world and what a pity we shall never be there to see it evolve into a world that shall be governed and controlled by little kids and their deep acumen at the cyber.

Abhishek often feels a bit frustrated when he is unable to spend much time with his daughter due to his busy work schedule. 'When I was growing up, Dad was hardly around because he was busy shooting. But he made it a point to be

India's most famous baby, Aaradhya, with her mother.

Aishwarya and Abhishek at the 62nd Cannes Film Festival, May 2009.

there when I needed him. I will also try to do the same for Aaradhya,' he said in a recent interview. He noted, 'Aish is always there for Aaradhya and so she is doing everything for her. I have nothing much to do. She always keeps talking to her and keeps teaching her all the poems and the other entire essential things. So, I just have to be with her and keep enjoying what she murmurs.' The baby is the focus of everyone in the Bachchan household: 'Everybody is fascinated with her. She is little and innocent and everybody wants to be with her, everyone wants to spend time with her.'

Aishwarya is my buddy, a friend, confesses Abhishek.

Abhishek and Aishwarya are often asked about the future plans for Aaradhya to which Abhishek replies, 'It is too early to discuss her professional life. Undoubtedly, Aishwarya and I have no expectations about her joining the filmy arena. This one thing, I believe, should be left to the individual. Whatever Aaradhya would love to do, we will both support her as parents.'

As for now, she is responsible for keeping the Bachchan families on their toes, a fact that is evident in one of the entries in her grandfather's blog, 'Never realised playing with the "little one" for just a few minutes could be equivalent to an entire two-hour workout in the gym! Child is the father of man.'

Individually each of them is different, independent, with a persona of their own. They are all stalwarts in their own space but, when together as a family, they are committed to 'Being a Bachchan'. For Abhishek, 'Going back to a happy, healthy family at the end of the day is more important than being successful.' They are known to be a close-knit family, despite having different personalities and habits. Says Abhishek:

Left to right: Amitabh, Shweta, Anil Kapoor, Sonam Kapoor, Manish Malhotra, Farhan Akhtar, Javed Akhtar, Shatrugan Sinha, Sonakshi Sinha, Jaya and Abhishek.

I am more like my mother than my father; in fact, I even act like her. I am a people's person like her. I am very outgoing. My dad is a loner. He likes to have us around. He would call us in his study and we used to sit there for hours without saying a word. We were never brought up like star kids. We were any other normal family.

The Bachchans appreciate each other's professional liabilities and commitments but, despite their busy schedules, keep in touch through technology. At times they ping just to inform that one of them is stuck in a traffic jam or sometimes the ping is an odd request of feeling like having chaat! But no matter what, they make time to have meals together, whenever possible. Jaya has made a rule that if they are in Mumbai, they should at least have one meal of the day together. Amitabh once remarked, 'The name Bachchan means a lot to me. I hope I have maintained the respectability that I have inherited and it will be strengthened by Abhishek and carried forward by my grandchildren.'

THE FATHER, THE SON & THE COLOSSAL SHADOW

BY VIKAS CHANDRA SINHA

Sons have often felt challenged by the success of their iconic fathers once they embark on their careers. In 1972, Australia was engulfed by a bizarre and sad development in the life of Sir Donald George Bradman, universally revered as the greatest cricketer ever. His only son, John Bradman, 32, changed his last name to Bradsen by deed poll after struggling for years with the most recognisable name in Australia.

John felt the compelling need to step out of his father's shadow. He explained himself in a newspaper article, 'I'm tired of people "discovering" who I am. I'm me. And I am no longer prepared to accept being seriously introduced as simply someone's son. I'm an individual not a social souvenir. I was popped into a metaphorical glass cage to be peered at and discussed like the other exhibits.' John wasn't even in the same profession as his father. He stayed away from cricket and made a career as a lecturer in environmental and constitutional

Abhishek has borne his father's shadow with an equanimity that deserves appreciation

Photo courtesy: Vinod Krishnan

law. Nevertheless, he felt oppressed by his father's fame. It was not his fault. Sir Don Bradman was not just a successful sportsperson, he embodied the Australian national identity and continues to do so.

Iconic 'epoch making' fathers such as Bradman present unique challenges to their grown-up children. A different dynamic operates in such cases and a father's success can cast a colossal shadow that is simply impossible to shake off, no matter how hard one tries. Abhishek finds himself in a similar predicament. His father is the gold standard against which every Indian actor measures himself, in Bollywood or in similarly named numerous other 'woods' that reflect the diversity and depth of film culture in our country. Amitabh has come to symbolise Hindi cinema globally, so much so that even his 'blink and you miss' Hollywood debut in *The Great Gatsby* was commented upon across the world. The brevity of his role was fodder to reemphasise his greatness. *The Wall Street Journal* ran an interview with Rachel Dwyer, professor of Indian culture and cinema at the School of Oriental and African Studies, London, on its website. Dwyer analysed Amitabh's Hollywood debut, 'I would also think that the people in Hollywood, who had heard of Mr Bachchan, would know that he is not just another star and they may well have felt it would not be appropriate to cast him as anything other than a leading hero.'

The father and son have always shared a very close relationship, a fact endorsed by this cover story.

Amitabh Bachchan is an 'era defining' actor who has defined not one but many eras in Bollywood. After a barren initiation, he turned the industry upside down by inaugurating the 'angry young man' in the 1970s and 80s. As the Khans took over in the 1990s, Amitabh broke a taboo and crossed over to television, revolutionising evening entertainment with 'Kaun Banega Crorepati', which has spawned numerous quiz and reality shows that have changed Indian television forever. Movie stars today no longer feel that exposure to television will lessen their mystique and, in fact, are quite keen to appear on television, especially to promote their films. Just when Amitabh was becoming the favourite grandfatherly television quizmaster for a young India in the early part of this century, he returned to the film industry with an astonishing second wind signalled by a creative burst that has seen him enact a diversity of roles that have left the audience asking for more. His repertoire in his second coming, featuring films across genres (*Bunty Aur Babli*, *Sarkar, Paa, Black, Cheeni Kum, The Last Lear* to *Piku*) equals—if not surpasses—his output from his glory days as the 'one man industry'. In an industry that is famously partial to youth, having such a body of work so late in his career is an achievement par excellence.

Abhishek's travails as a star son have been well-documented. *Business Standard* called him 'neither as celebrated as Hrithik Roshan or Ranbir Kapoor nor as spectacular a letdown as Fardeen Khan or Tusshar Kapoor, a star son stuck somewhere in the middle of the popularity race'. While adequately capturing Abhishek's mid-table ranking as a star, it ignored one profound truth. None of the other mentioned star sons had a father who enveloped their careers like a banyan tree. And we all know the truism that nothing grows under a banyan tree. At the beginning of their careers, all the other star sons could have reasonably hoped to match or exceed their father's success and popularity. Not so Abhishek. He knew from the start that he could not match his father's stardom: 'I will never have success like my Dad. He is the biggest, was, is and is ever going to be. So [I] don't aspire to be that because it is not going to happen.' It is hence futile to put him in the same bracket as other star sons.

There is no denying that Abhishek's record is decidedly mixed with a few highs and many lows. But even if he had been more successful, in the eyes of the world he would still have fallen short of his father and been compared unfavourably. Amitabh voiced this sentiment when he said, 'As an actor, I feel bad for Abhishek at times because he is a very good actor; just that he is not getting his due.' Consider the case of the hockey legend Dhyan Chand and his

Watching Amitabh and Abhishek perform together is always a treat for Bachchan fans.

Amitabh is an 'era defining' actor who has defined not one but many eras in Bollywood.

illustrious son Ashok Kumar. Dhyan Chand, like Bradman, is considered the greatest exponent of his sport. He is unarguably India's greatest sportsperson who probably deserved to be the first person from the field of sports to be awarded the Bharat Ratna, ahead of Sachin Tendulkar. He was so magical on the hockey field that his exploits have entered folklore, with Amar Chitra Katha bringing out a comic book on him. In an article in *Live Mint*, Kumar recalls the constant murmurs that accompanied his travels—'that's Dhyan Chand's son'—and that he felt pressured to perform because people expected him to. And perform he did, Ashok Kumar was part of the only Indian team ever to win the World Cup in hockey in 1975. He played a stellar role in that win, scoring the only goal in the final against Pakistan, but most people recall him as his father's son and some regret that he was not as good as him.

Abhishek's record is decidedly mixed with a few highs and many lows.

Families monopolising success is fairly common in the fields of business, music, the arts, sports and politics. Whether it is down to 'nature' (that is, innate talent, genetics and so on) or 'nurture' (practice, congenial environment and so on) has long been a topic of debate in psychology. Opining in favour of the strivers, Malcolm Gladwell made the '10,000-hour rule' famous in his book *Outliers*. He observed that practice is 'the thing you do that makes you good' and isn't 'the thing you do once you're good'. Contrarily, research also points that in domains of virtuosity, striving and innate talent both matter. There are many born with talent but they have to complement it with a work ethic and those who do, have an edge over those who don't. But the converse is not true; those with less talent can hardly make up the deficit with practice. And in physically-driven fields, such as sports, films or music, talent is mostly

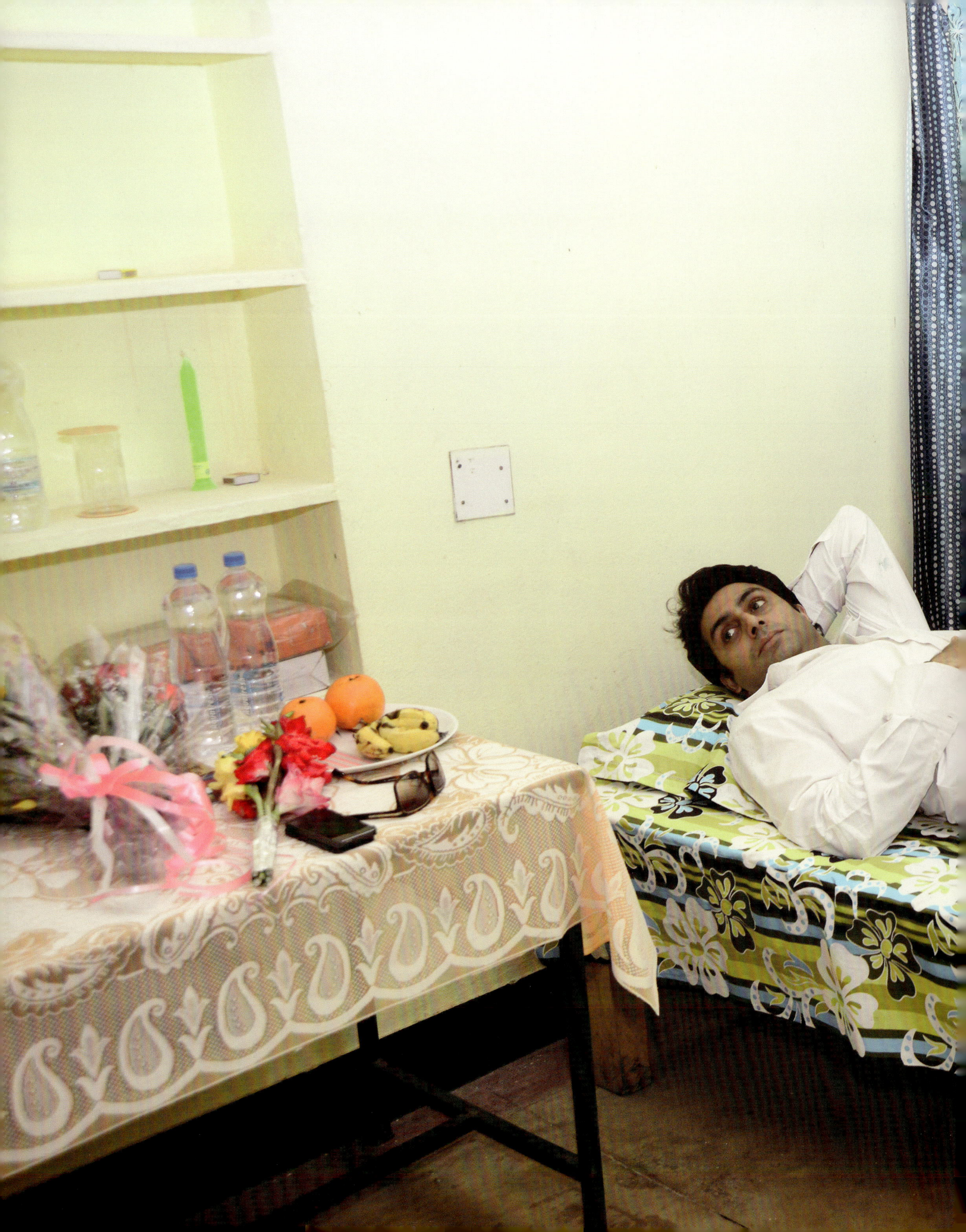

inherited, ensuring that success runs in families. The man on the street is aware of this but that does not sit well with ideas of meritocracy that most of us so prize. This explains why the general audience has an ambivalent and contradictory attitude towards star children. A star child's debut is greeted with anticipation and s/he is probably afforded more chances as people assume that they are talented but, on the flip side, the criticism, when it comes, can be sharp, unrelenting and personal. Audiences across the world have a love-hate relationship with dynasties—in sports or films or any other sphere of activity.

Could this love-hate relationship be the reason why, in the Hindi film industry, no two male members of the same family have been big stars simultaneously? The audience is willing to reward the talented star child but, in a nod to meritocracy, withholds its affection to more than one from the same family at any given time. Sounds fanciful, but consider the first family of Hindi cinema. The Kapoors have provided an endless stream of stars to Bollywood starting with Prithviraj Kapoor in the 1930s and 40s, one of the first genuine Indian movie stars. But Raj ascended to stardom as Prithviraj was turning back to his first love, theatre, in the late 1940s. Shammi announced his superstardom to the world with his *Junglee* moment but, by then, Raj was more 'showman' than 'superstar', concentrating on producing and directing movies. Shashi's best moments were after Shammi had moved on to character roles. Rishi and Shashi briefly shone together but Shashi went on to producing landmark films, leaving Rishi as the sole shining Kapoor scion. And now Ranbir has arrived to take forward the Kapoor legacy. The point to note is that it was only one big male star from the Kapoor family at any given point in time, even though the failed Kapoors such as Randhir, Kunal or Chimpu all showed some talent and were received well at the outset of their careers.

The case of Dharmendra and his sons is similar. Sunny made his debut when Dharmendra's career was winding down. Bobby made his when Sunny was at the height of his powers. In spite of a strong initial showing, Bobby fizzled out. In the case of Abhishek, his father's career has actually got stronger after his debut. His first film, *Refugee*, released in July 2000, within weeks of Amitabh's game-changing television debut with 'Kaun Banega Crorepati'. While Abhishek struggled, Amitabh went from strength to strength. If the audience has had to ration its affection between the two Bachchans, it is

Previous page: Taking time out from a hectic schedule to relax.

The Bachchan surname has been an asset and a liability in equal measure for Abhishek.

natural that Abhishek has got the smaller share. Maybe Abhishek deserves more credit than he is given just for carving an individual niche for himself.

A star child's debut normally creates anticipation all around. And, if the parent is as big as Amitabh, this anticipation can be heady. Bhawna Somaya, writing in *The Hindu* about Abhishek's debut movie, called the anticipation 'unprecedented, something unheard of in the past 20 years':

> I saw the film first day first show at Chandan theatre in Juhu [Mumbai] and spotted familiar faces in the audience, eager to check the newcomer's credentials. The experience was enchanting. Abhishek's introductory scene was welcomed with whistles and when he delivered his first dialogue, in a voice so similar to his father, the auditorium resounded with claps. [They] unanimously cheered the new hero. It was the kind of reaction you see during live performance on stage.

The Bachchans with Manisha Koirala and Gulshan Grover at the Big Star Entertainment Awards ceremony.

Why does so much hullabaloo accompany a star child? The audience probably looks forward to re-experiencing the mystique of a much loved bygone star. But, in Abhishek's case, the mystique of his father never faded—there was nothing for him to recreate, rather it was easier for the audience to compare his prowess with his father's. In many of his better movies and commercial successes, he shared screen space with his dad and, not surprisingly, came out second best. Producers felt that casting the father and son combination was a coup and a safer bet commercially but, perhaps, these films pushed Abhishek further into his father's shadow.

Rishi Kapoor once said in a lighter vein that one of his achievements as an actor was to 'survive Amitabh Bachchan'. He was, of course, referring to

Amitabh's vice-like dominance of the Hindi film industry. But this description is perhaps more apt for Abhishek. His career has been one saga of struggle with his father's colossal shadow, which probably has not allowed him to flower to the fullest extent possible. The word 'shadow' has been used in conjunction with his name more than any other celebrity's. The Bachchan surname has been an asset and a liability in equal measure for Abhishek. He has often had to answer questions about this. Shares Abhishek: 'At the premiere of my first film, director Yash Chopra told me, "Son, your father's name will bring people to your first show. They'll think that he's Amitabh Bachchan's son, let's check him out. But after that they'll come to see you only if you're good".'

And the criticism has been vicious when he has not been good. Anurag Kashyap tore into him, even when his performance was good in *Yuva*, suggesting that he had not understood half the lines he wrote for him and never rose above the script. Abhishek once said in an interview:

> ... every Friday when you open the papers and there's a review of your film and instead of reviewing the film, they reviewed you personally. As a young actor, it gets to you and it did to me as well. You know initially the first two or three films you try and develop a thick skin and say, ok fine, you know. But then when it happens repeatedly, it starts to get to you. You start believing it.

Elsewhere, he has commented, '... after a while I became numb. I began watching the process from a distance, like an outsider.'

Many contend that it is the surname that has allowed the junior Bachchan to get a foothold in the industry. Critics point out that he faced 17 flops before he could deliver a hit; yet he has managed to star in more than 50 films as lead or second lead of which roughly four-fifths have been commercial flops. Abhishek is acutely aware of such sentiments and has expressed his anguish:

> People allege that I've survived in this industry because I am my father's son. I have a question to ask them—'If producers want to sign my father then they should cast him. Why would they want to cast me?' No one is doing charity here. How can I expect people to spend a few hundred rupees to watch my film because I am someone's son?

The Bachchans were delightful to watch in Paa.

The irony is that Amitabh has never overtly pushed his son's career. Unlike many star fathers, he has not made any film for him. 'In fact, I made *Paa* for him,' Abhishek once joked.

People sympathetic to Abhishek talk about the stellar performances that he has delivered in *Refugee, Yuva, Bunty Aur Babli* and *Sarkar*. They also suggest that it was sheer bad luck that some of his well-crafted and well-acted movies such as *Delhi-6, Khelein Hum Jee Jaan Sey* and *Raavan* could not capture the imagination of the audience. With *Guru*, Abhishek has certainly shown that, in the hands of a good director, he can deliver a complete performance second to none. As his commercial flops piled up, he stopped getting such projects, limiting his ability to show his métier. He has continued to shine, though, in films with ensemble casts such as *Bol Bachchan*, the *Dhoom* series and *Happy New Year*. Abhishek, the actor, has earned his spurs but question marks continue to hang over Abhishek, the star.

And the debate goes on. Would any other actor in his place, especially an outsider to the industry, have got so many opportunities to prove himself the way Abhishek got? Is Abhishek an underrated actor with his father's shadow hanging over him? Is he a talented actor who has not done justice to his talent because of his choice of films? Is he a good actor who is judged harshly because of his background?

Wherever one may stand in this discussion, it is undeniable that Abhishek has borne his father's shadow with an equanimity that deserves appreciation. There has been no Bradman-style rebellion against his father's unmatchable legacy. John Bradman took a lifetime to reconcile with his father's shadow, finally reclaiming his surname just before his father's death. Abhishek has remained remarkably sanguine about the enormous expectations and also the whispers about unfair privilege that accompany him constantly by virtue of being his father's son: 'I am lucky and proud to carry the Bachchan surname. I feel I am over appreciated,' he declares. There is much to learn from him.

Vikas Chandra Sinha is an IIT and IIM alumnus who finds Abhishek's struggles inspirational

POEM

by Hemant Kumar 'Dhaakad'

अनुपम हैं कहते सभी, हैं लाखों में एक,
ऐश्वर्या-हसबैंड है, अमित-पुत्र अभिषेक।
अमित-पुत्र अभिषेक, करे हैं अभिनय सच्चा,
इनको करे पसंद, देश का बच्चा-बच्चा।
कह धाकड़ कविराय, विरासत इनकी उत्तम,
मातु-पिता से मिली, आपको प्रतिभा अनुपम॥

केवल अभिनय ही नहीं करें और भी काम,
खेलों को आगे करें, दे कर पूरे दाम।
देकर पूरे दाम, बढ़े फुटबॉल कबड्डी,
और नशे से बचे, रहे ना देश फिसड्डी।
कह धाकड़ कविराय, बढ़ाएँ सबका लेवल,
और बढ़ें अभिषेक, दौर शुरुआती केवल॥

He is exceptional, ingenious,
everyone's Abhishek

Aishwarya's constant companion,
splendid Amit's lad

Splendid Amit's lad, his grand
acting immensely we enjoy

Sweetheart of the nation, love
of every girl and boy

Declares the smashing bard—
his legacy is incredibly fine

From his mother and father he
got the flair to shine

Acting is just one thing for him,
he has vocations many

Disburses his resources generously,
sports he likes any

Disburses his means kindly,
encourages kabaddi, football

Dodges intoxication, so that
nation progresses, not crawls

Declares the smashing bard—
he lifts everyone's level

Luck be with you Abhishek,
your aura remains stable.

translated by
Rachna Agrawal

A painting of Abhishek, showing the shadow of Amitabh and signature of his grandfather, by artist Rajesh Srivastava.

FILMOGRAPHY

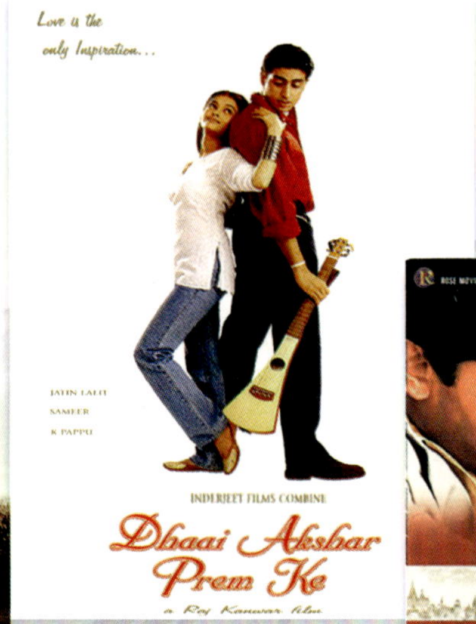

YEAR	FILM	ROLE	CO-STARRING
2000	Refugee	Refugee	Kareena Kapoor, Sunil Shetty, Jackie Shroff, Kulbhushan Kharbanda
2000	Tera Jadoo Chal Gayaa	Kabir Srivastav	Keerti Reddy, Sanjay Suri, Kader Khan, Paresh Rawal
2000	Dhaai Akshar Prem Ke	Karan Khanna	Aishwarya Rai, Amrish Puri, Anupam Kher
2001	Bas Itna Sa Khwaab Hai	Surajchand C Shrivastav	Rani Mukerji, Jackie Shroff, Sushmita Sen, Gulshan Grover
2002	Haan Maine Bhi Pyaar Kiya	Shiv Kapoor	Akshay Kumar, Karisma Kapoor, Kader Khan, Simone Singh, Shakti Kapoor
2002	Shararat	Rahul Khanna	Hrishitaa Bhatt, Om Puri, Amrish Puri, Helen, Tinnu Anand
2002	Om Jai Jagadish	Jagadish Batra	Anil Kapoor, Fardeen Khan, Mahima Choudhary, Urmila Matondkar, Diya Mirza
2002	Desh	Anjaan	Jaya Bachchan, Abhishek Bachchan
2003	Kuch Naa Kaho	Raj	Aishwarya Rai, Satish Shah, Parth Dave, Himani Shivpuri, Suhasini Mulay
2003	Zameen	ACP Jaideep 'Jai' Rai	Ajay Devgn, Bipasha Basu, Mukesh Tiwari

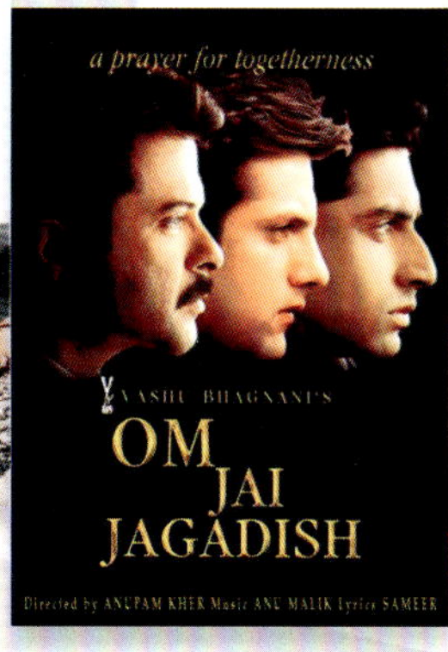

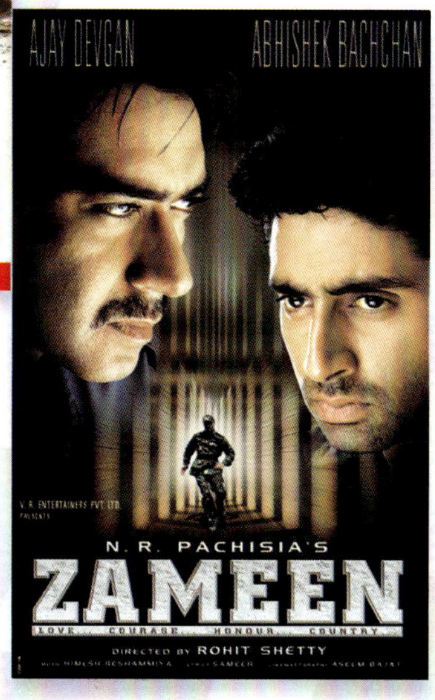

Director	Producer	Story	Screenplay/Dialogue	Music
JP Dutta	JP Dutta, Rajesh Bhatt (executive producer)	JP Dutta	JP Dutta, OP Dutta	Anu Malik, Adesh Shrivastava
A Muthu	Vashu Bhagnani, Khemchand Bhagnani (executive producer)	Ikram Akhtar	Ikram Akhtar	Ranjit Barot, Ismail Darbar
Raj Kanwar	Raj Kanwar, K Pappu (co-producer), Amardeep Singh (executive producer)	Raj Kanwar	Jainendra Jain	Jatin Pandit, Lalit Pandit, Naresh Sharma
Goldie Behl	Madhu Ramesh Behl	Goldie Behl	Goldie Behl, Tigmanshu Dhulia (dialogue)	Adesh Shrivastava
Dharmesh Darshan	Suneel Darshan	Raj Sinha	Dharmesh Darshan, Naseem Mukri (dialogue), Raj Sinha	Nadeem Shravan, Surendra Singh Sodhi
Gurudev Bhalla	Gurudev Bhalla, Suraj Bhalla (executive producer)	Urmi Juvekar	Tanveer Khan	Babloo Chakravorty
Anupam Kher	Vashu Bhagnani, Khemchand Bhagnani (executive producer)	Rahul Nanda	Rumi Jaffery	Ranjit Barot, Anu Malik
Raja Sen	Ramesh Gandhi	Animesh Rai Chaudhary	Animesh Rai Chaudhary	
Rohan Sippy	Ramesh Sippy, Hussain Shaikh (executive producer)	Rohena Gera	Naushil Mehta, Nidhi Tuli (dialogue), Neeraj Vora (screenplay)	Shankar-Ehsaan-Loy, Aadesh Shrivastava, Uday Mazumdar
Rohit Shetty	NR Pachisia	Suparn Verma	Suparn Verma, Javed Siddiqui (dialogue)	Himesh Reshammiya

YEAR	FILM	ROLE	CO-STARRING
2003	Main Prem Ki Diwani Hoon	Prem Kumar	Hrithik Roshan, Kareena Kapoor, Pankaj Kapur, Himani Shivpuri, Johnny Lever
2003	Mumbai Se Aaya Mera Dost	Kanji	Lara Dutta, Chunkey Pandey, Aditya Lakhia, Yashpal Sharma, Daya Shankar Pandey
2003	LOC Kargil	Lt. Vikram Batra	Ajay Devgn, Akshaye Khanna, Sanjay Dutt, Saif Ali Khan, Sunil Shetty
2004	Naach	Abhinav	Antara Mali, Riteish Deshmukh
2004	Yuva	Lallan Singh	Ajay Devgn, Vivek Oberoi, Esha Deol, Kareena Kapoor, Rani Mukerji
2004	Run	Siddharth 'Sidhu' Varma	Bhoomika Chawla, Mahesh Manjrekar, Ayesha Julka, Mukesh Rishi, Vijay Raaz
2004	Phir Milenge	Advocate Tarun Anand	Salman Khan, Shilpa Shetty
2004	Dhoom	ACP Jai Dixit	John Abraham, Uday Chopra, Esha Deol, Rimi Sen
2005	Bunty Aur Babli	Rakesh Trivedi/ Bunty	Rani Mukerji, Amitabh Bachchan, Tania Zaetta
2005	Sarkar	Shankar Nagre	Amitabh Bachchan, Abhishek Bachchan, Kay Kay Menon, Rukhsar Rehman, Kota Srinivasa Rao, Katrina Kaif, Tanisha Mukherjee, Anupam Kher
2005	Dus	Shashank Dheer	Sanjay Dutt, Sunil Shetty, Zayed Khan, Shilpa Shetty, Esha Deol

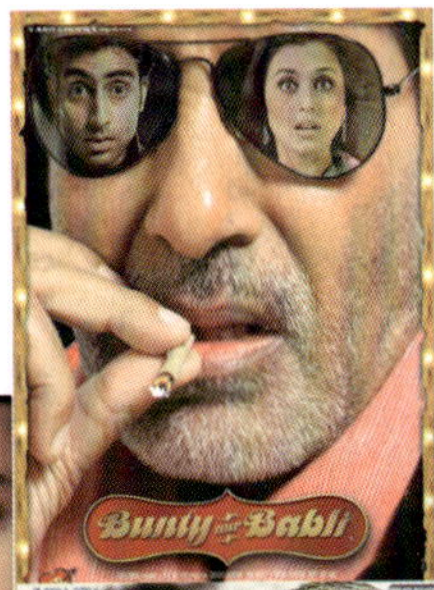

DIRECTOR	PRODUCER	STORY	SCREENPLAY/DIALOGUE	MUSIC
Sooraj R Barjatya	Ajit Kumar Barjatya, Kamal Kumar Barjatya, Rajkumar Barjatya	Sooraj R Barjatya	Sooraj R Barjatya	Anu Malik
Apoorva Lakhia	Vishal Nihalani (producer), Chirag Nihalani, Deepesh Nihalani, Laxmi Singh (executive producer)	Apoorva Lakhia	Apoorva Lakhia	Ranjit Barot, Anu Malik, Amar Mohile
JP Dutta	Rajesh Bhatt, Bindiya Goswami (executive producer)	JP Dutta	OP Dutta	Anu Malik
Ram Gopal Varma	Namrata Oberoi, Chitra Subramaniam (executive producer), Ram Gopal Varma (co-producer)	Sulekha Bajpai, Musharaff Ali Khan	Sulekha Bajpai, Musharaff Ali Khan	Suleiman Merchant, Amar Mohile, Shailendra Swapnil
Mani Ratnam	Mani Ratnam, G Srinivasan	Based on Tamil film *Aaytha Ezhuthu*	Anurag Kashyap (dialogue), Mani Ratnam (screenplay)	AR Rahman
Jeeva	Boney Kapoor, Sridevi	N Linguswamy	Kamal Pandey	Himesh Reshammiya
Revathy	Sarita Patil (executive producer), Suresh Balaje, George Pius Tharayil (line producer)	Atul Sabharwal	Atul Sabharwal	Shankar-Ehsaan-Loy, Bhavatha Raja, Nikhil-Vinay. Lyrics: Prasoon Joshi
Sanjay Gadhvi	Aditya Chopra, Yash Chopra (producer), Shahnaab Alam (executive producer)	Aditya Chopra	Vijay Krishna Acharya	Pritam, Salim Suleiman
Shaad Ali	Aditya Chopra and Yash Chopra (producer), Sanjay Shivalkar (executive producer)	Aditya Chopra	Jaideep Sahni	Shankar-Ehsaan-Loy
Ram Gopal Varma	Parag Sanghavi, Ram Gopal Varma	RR Venkat Rao (executive producer)	Ram Gopal Varma	Amar Mohile
Anubhav Sinha	Sohail Maklai and Nitin Manmohan (producer), Kalim Khan (executive producer)	Anubhav Sinha	Vinay and Yash	Ranjit Barot, Vishal Shekhar

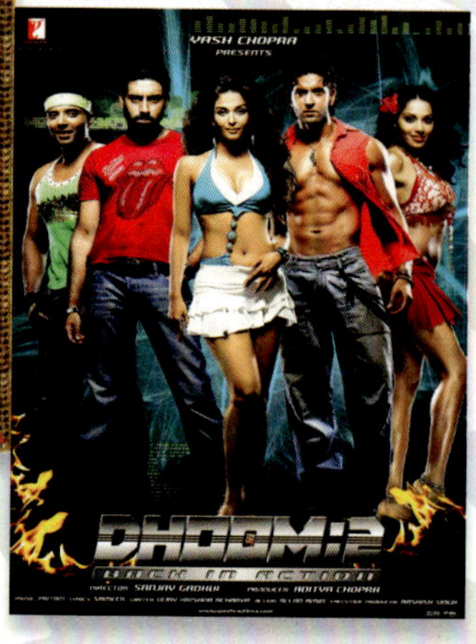

YEAR	FILM	ROLE	CO-STARRING
2005	Antarmahal	Brij Bhushan	Jackie Shroff, Raima Sen, Soha Ali Khan, Roopa Ganguly
2005	Bluffmaster	Roy Kapoor	Priyanka Chopra, Riteish Deshmukh, Nana Patekar, Boman Irani
2006	Kabhi Alvida Naa Kehna	Rishi Talwar	Amitabh Bachchan, Shah Rukh Khan, Rani Mukerji, Preity Zinta, Kirron Kher
2006	Umrao Jaan	Nawab Sultan	Aishwarya Rai, Sunil Shetty, Shabana Azmi, Divya Dutta, Himani Shivpuri
2006	Dhoom 2	ACP Jai Dixit	Hrithik Roshan, Aishwarya Rai, Bipasha Basu, Uday Chopra, Rimi Sen
2007	Guru	Gurukant Desai	Aishwarya Rai, Vidya Balan, R Madhavan, Mallika Sherawat, Mithun Chakraborty
2007	Shootout At Lokhandwala	Sub-Inspector Abhishek Mahatre	Amitabh Bachchan, Sanjay Dutt, Tusshar Kapoor, Vivek Oberoi, Arbaaz Khan, Rohit Roy
2007	Jhoom Barabar Jhoom	Rakesh 'Ricky' Thakral	Amitabh Bachchan, Bobby Deol, Preity Zinta, Lara Dutta
2007	Laaga Chunari Mein Daag	Rohan Varma	Jaya Bachchan, Rani Mukerji, Konkona Sen Sharma, Kunal Kapoor, Anupam Kher
2008	Sarkar Raj	Shankar Nagre	Amitabh Bachchan, Aishwarya Rai, Tanisha Mukherjee, Victor Banerjee, Govind Namdeo
2008	Drona	Aditya 'Adi'/Drona	Jaya Bachchan, Priyanka Chopra, Kay Kay Menon

DIRECTOR	PRODUCER	STORY	SCREENPLAY/DIALOGUE	MUSIC
Rituparno Ghosh	Jaya Bachchan and Vashu Bhagnani (producer), Anil Kuriakose (executive producer)	Tarashankar Banerjee	Rituparno Ghosh	Debajyoti Mishra
Rohan Sippy	Ramesh Sippy (producer), Hussain Shaikh (executive producer)	Shridhar Raghavan	Rajat Arora (dialogue), Shridhar Raghavan (screenplay)	Vishal Shekhar
Karan Johar	Hiroo Johar (producer), Anadil Hossain and Manoj Mittra (executive producer)	Karan Johar	Shibani Bathija and Karan Johar (screenplay), Niranjan Iyengar (dialogue)	Shankar-Ehsaan-Loy
JP Dutta	JP Dutta (producer), Rajesh Bhatt (executive producer)	OP Dutta	JP Dutta	Anu Malik
Sanjay Gadhvi	Aditya Chopra, Yash Chopra (producer), Aashish Singh (executive producer)	Aditya Chopra	Vijay Krishna Acharya	Pritam
Mani Ratnam	Mani Ratnam, G. Srinivasan (producer)	Mani Ratnam	Mani Ratnam (screenplay), Vijay Krishna Acharya (dialogue)	AR Rahman
Apoorva Lakhia	Sanjay Gupta, Ekta Kapoor, Shobha Kapoor (producer)	Sanjay Gupta, Suresh Nair, Apoorva Lakhia	Raj Vasant (dialogue)	Anand Raj Anand, Biddu, Euphoria, Shibani Kashyap, Mika Singh
Shaad Ali	Aditya Chopra, Yash Chopra (producer), Sanjay Shivalkar (executive producer)	Anurag Kashyap	Habib Faisal	Shankar-Ehsaan-Loy
Pradeep Sarkar	Aditya Chopra and Pradeep Sarkar (producer), Swaratmika Mishra (executive producer)	Aditya Chopra	Rekha Nigam	Shantanu Moitra
Ram Gopal Varma	Praveen Nischol and Ram Gopal Varma (producer)	Prashant Pandey	Prashant Pandey (dialogue), Ram Gopal Varma (screenplay)	Bapi-Tutul
Goldie Behl	Shrishti Behl, Sunil Lulla (producer)	Goldie Behl	Rohini Killough, Jaydeep Sarkar (screenplay)	Dhruv Ghanekar

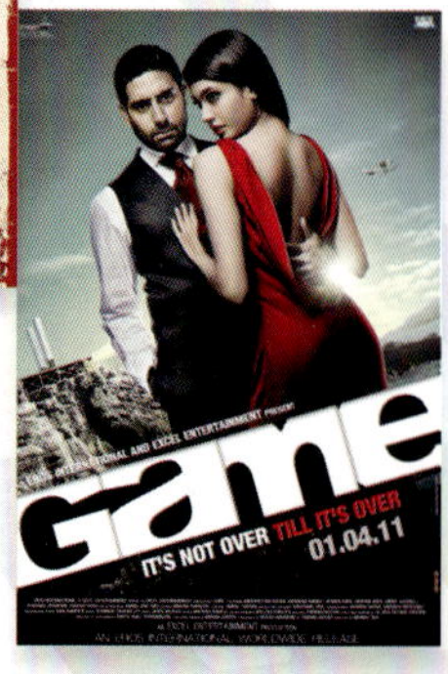

YEAR	FILM	ROLE	CO-STARRING
2008	Dostana	Sameer 'Sam' Acharya	John Abraham, Priyanka Chopra, Kirron Kher, Boman Irani
2009	Delhi-6	Roshan Mehra	Sonam Kapoor, Rishi Kapoor, Waheeda Rehman, Atul Kulkarni, Supriya Pathak
2009	Paa	Amol Arte	Amitabh Bachchan, Vidya Balan, Paresh Rawal, Arundhati Naag, Taruni Sachdeva
2010	Raavan	Beera Munda	Aishwarya Rai, Govinda, Manisha Koirala, Chiyaan Vikram
2010	Khelein Hum Jee Jaan Sey	Surjya Sen	Deepika Padukone, Sikander Kher, Vishakha Singh, Samrat Mukherji, Maninder Singh
2011	Game	Neil Menon	Sarah Jane Dias, Boman Irani, Jimmy Shergill, Gul Panag, Shahana Goswami
2011	Dum Maaro Dum	ACP Vishnu Kamath	Aditya Pancholi, Bipasha Basu, Rana Daggubati, Prateik Babbar, Gantois Gomes
2012	Players	Charlie Masceranhas	Sonam Kapoor, Bobby Deol, Bipasha Basu, Neil Nitin Mukesh, Omi Vaidya
2012	Bol Bachchan	Abbas Ali/ Abhishek Bachchan	Ajay Devgn, Asin Thottumkal, Prachi Desai, Asrani, Krishna
2013	Dhoom 3	ACP Jai Dixit	Aamir Khan, Uday Chopra, Katrina Kaif, Jackie Shroff
2014	Happy New Year	Nandu Bhide/ Vicky Grover	Shah Rukh Khan, Deepika Padukone, Sonu Sood, Boman Irani, Vivaan Shah
2015	All Is Well	Inder Bhalla	Asin Thottumkal, Rishi Kapoor, Supriya Pathak

DIRECTOR	PRODUCER	STORY	SCREENPLAY/DIALOGUE	MUSIC
Tarun Mansukhani	Hiroo Johar, Karan Johar (producer)	Tarun Mansukhani	Anvita Dutt Guptan	Vishal and Shekhar
Rakeysh Omprakash Mehra	Rakeysh Omprakash Mehra, Ronnie Screwvala (producer)	Rakeysh Omprakash Mehra, Prasoon Joshi, Kamlesh Pandey	Rakeysh Omprakash Mehra, Prasoon Joshi, Kamlesh Pandey	AR Rahman
R Balki	Sunil Manchanda (producer)	R Balki	R Balki	Ilayaraja
Mani Ratnam	Mani Ratnam, Sharada Trilok (producer)	Suhasini	Mani Ratnam (screenplay), Vijay Krishna Acharya (dialogue)	AR Rahman
Ashutosh Gowariker	Ajay Bijli, Sanjeev K Bijli, Sunita Gowariker (producer)	Based on Manini Chatterjee's novel	Ashutosh Gowariker and Raoul Randolf (screenplay), Vijay Maurya (dialogue)	Sohail Sen
Abhinay Deo	Farhan Akhtar, Ritesh Sidhwani (producer)	Althea Delmas Kaushal	Althea Delmas Kaushal, Farhan Akhtar (dialogue)	Shankar-Ehsaan-Loy
Rohan Sippy	Ramesh Sippy (producer)	Shridhar Raghavan	Charudutt Acharya, Purva Naresh, Shridhar Raghavan (dialogue)	Pritam
Abbas-Mastan	Pappu Vaswani, Mohammed Burmawala	Nikhat Bhatty, Bhaskar Hazarika, Sourabh Ratnu	Sudip Sharma, Rohit Jugraj (screenplay)	Pritam Chakraborty, Sandeep Shirodkar
Rohit Shetty	Ajay Devgn, Dhilin Mehta (producer)	Rohit Shetty	Farhad and Sajid (dialogue), Yunus Sajawal (screenplay)	Atul Gogavale, Himesh Reshammiya
Vijay Krishna Acharya	Aditya Chopra (producer)	Vijay Krishna Acharya	Vijay Krishna Acharya, Aditya Chopra	Pritam
Farah Khan	Gauri Khan, Karuna Badwal	Farah Khan	Farah Khan, Althea Kaushal, Mayur Puri (dialogue)	Vishal and Shekhar, John Stewart Eduri
Umesh Shukla	Shyam Bajaj, Varun Bajaj, Bhushan Kumar, Krishan Kumar	Sumit Arora, Niren Bhatt	Sumit Arora, Niren Bhatt	Meet Brothers, Anjjan, Amaal Malik, Mithoon, Himesh Reshammiya

SPECIAL APPEARANCE OF ABHISHEK BACHCHAN

Year/Film

2004
Rakht

2004
Hum Tum

2005
Salaam Namaste

2005
Neal 'n' Nikki

2005
Home Delivery

2005
Ek Ajnabee

2007
Ram Gopal Varma Ki Aag

2006
Lage Raho Munna Bhai

2006
Alag

2008
Mission Istaanbul

2015
Shamitabh

Acknowledgements

At the outset, my special thanks to Abhishek Bachchan for his consent to my book. The Bachchan family has also been supportive and I warmly acknowledge their contribution. Jayaji has given her kind permission to use photographs from her book. Bachchan Senior has always encouraged me and sent his *shubh kaamnaiyen* whenever I texted him about the progress of my book.

I am thankful to my former editor at *Bombay Times*, Malavika Sangghvi, for writing the foreword. I am also grateful to the guest writers—Ayaz Memon, Narendra Kusnur, Vikas Chandra Sinha—for their contributions and inputs. Hemant Kumar 'Dhaakar' has written a special poem on the actor, which adds lustre to my book.

The pictures used in the book are primarily the ones I have photographed over the years. Additionally I have used pictures shot by my friends and fellow colleagues. I thank Amol Kamble, Dinodia Photo Agency, Fotocorp, Dashrath Kadam, Umesh Goswamy and Siddhant Gill for happily sharing their images with me. In the chapter 'Starting Young' all images are courtesy the book *To Be or Not to Be*; I thank Jayaji for graciously allowing the use of these images.

This book would not have been completed without the film stills and this was made possible by the producers of Abhishek Bachchan films. My thanks to all these production houses.

I also owe a special note of thanks to all those people who helped me with the research and interviews—in this regard I would like to mention SMM Ausaja for his valuable inputs. I am indebted to fellow artists who have contributed to this book—Rajesh Srivastava for doing a special painting, Mithun Singh for illustrating the chapter 'Being an Actor', Ganesh Shinde for his collage work and Nilesh Vede for his art work.

I also thank Write Media for editing and designing the book, Priyanka Chandra Sinha for all her editorial assistance and Saroj Gupta for the filmography.

Balakrishna Pillai (Spin Communique) has been a pillar of support throughout ... thanks, my friend. And, not to forget my friend, Dr Ram Jawhrani, who has always been extremely supportive.

My publishers, Bikash and Tultul Niyogi, have shown tremendous enthusiasm and patience during the creation of this work. They have been very encouraging and have always supported my projects.

Last, but not the least, I owe a debt of gratitude to my wife Veena Chandra for enduring my obsession with Abhishek Bachchan for an extended period.

Sources

Resources referred to in this book:

STARTING YOUNG

To Be or Not to Be—Book on Amitabh Bachchan

Bombay Times

BEING AN ACTOR

Screen

Bombay Times

Mid-Day

Filmfare

India Today

Showtime

Hi! Blitz

Stardust

Hindustan Times

DNA After Hrs.

DNA India

It List

HT Café

Matinee

GQ

Bollywood.com

Wikipedia

Bollywoodnaachgana.com

Timesofindia.com

Seasonsindia.com

IBNLive.com

Business-Standard.com

IMDB.com

Filmibeat.com

Tellychakkar.com

Rediff.com

Filmfare.com

Rajeevmasand.com

DIFFERENT GOALS

IBNlive.com

Indiawest.com

Rediff.com

Brainyquotes.com

Timesofindia.indiatimes.com

Thenational.ae

Premierleague.com

Bollywood.com

Celebrity.yahoo.com

Bombay Times

ALL IN THE FAMILY

Liveindia.com

Filmfare.com

Naachgaana.com

Bollywood.com

Timesofindia.indiatimes.com

Daily.bhaskar.com

IBNLive.com

Screen

Bombay Times

Mid-Day

Filmfare

India Today

Showtime

Hi! Blitz

Stardust

Hindustan Times

DNA After Hrs.

DNA India

It List

HT Café

Matinee

GQ

INDEX